A MUSIC LEARNING THEORY FOR NEWBORN AND YOUNG CHILDREN

G-3487

EDWIN E. GORDON
College of Music
Temple University

Carl E. Seashore Professor
for Research in Music Education

G.I.A. Publications, Inc.
Chicago

A Music Learning Theory
for Newborn and Young Children
by Edwin E. Gordon
Copyright © 1990 G.I.A. Publications, Inc.
7404 S. Mason Ave., Chicago, IL 60638
International copyright secured
Library of Congress Catalog Card Number: 90-071015
ISBN: 941050-23-8
Printed in U.S.A.

TABLE OF CONTENTS

Chapter Nine

A NOTE TO THE READER

In traditional usage the pronouns "he," "his," and "him" are often used to imply both sexes. As a result, the role of the female in society tends to be neglected. To deal with the problem by using double pronouns is not satisfactory; they become cumbersome for both the reader and the writer. Moreover, the use of plural nouns and pronouns often obscures specific meaning, as in the case of explaining how to teach to a child's individual musical needs. The practice undertaken in this book is to use the feminine and masculine pronouns in alternate chapters. Though it is probably not the best solution, the author hopes that the reader will accept it with sincerity and understanding.

On another matter, the Glossary should be called to the reader's attention. It is recommended that it be used frequently.

Chapter One

INTRODUCTION

Those who understand child development jest that they would like to die young as late as possible. They know that one's potential to learn is never greater than at the moment of birth. The most important time for learning in a child's life is from the day she is born (if not before) until she is three years old, a period during which she receives unstructured informal guidance in educational development. Next in importance is the time between the ages of three and five, a period during which the child receives structured informal guidance in educational development either at home or in preschool. What the child learns during the first five years of life forms the foundation for all subsequent educational development, which traditionally begins when she enters kindergarten or first grade and receives formal instruction. The younger the child is when that foundation is formed, the more she will profit from later instruction. The older the child is when that foundation is formed, the less she can profit from later instruction. There can be no correction for a lost opportunity to establish that foundation. Only compensatory instruction, not remedial instruction, is possible.

Remedial instruction and compensatory instruction are different. In a sense, remedial instruction is not possible. What was not developed in early life cannot be developed in later life to the extent that it could have been developed in early life. What has been lost cannot be recaptured. In compensatory instruction, all a teacher can do is to assist a child in progressing beyond whatever she brings to her formal schooling. All things being equal, a child who begins to learn at a later age will never learn as much as a child who begins to learn at an early age.

There is a difference between guidance and instruction in music. Regardless of type, all guidance is informal and all instruction is formal. Informal guidance can be either structured or unstructured. When guidance is unstructured, the parent or teacher does not plan specifically what she will say and do. When guidance is structured, the parent or teacher does plan specifically what she will say and do. A distinguishing characteristic of both structured and unstructured informal guidance, as compared to formal instruction, is that they do not impose information and skills upon the child. Rather, the child is exposed to her culture and encouraged to absorb that culture. Moreover, both structured and

1

unstructured informal guidance are based upon and carry forth the natural sequential activities and responses of the child. In formal instruction, in addition to the parent or teacher specifically planning what will be taught, teaching is organized into allotted time periods, and cooperation, including specific types of responses, is expected of the child.

The home is the most important school that young children will ever know, and their parents are the most important teachers that they will ever have. Most parents are more capable of guiding and instructing their children in the development of communication and arithmetic skills than of music skills. That is not necessarily because parents do not have high levels of music aptitudes. It is probably because most parents were not guided and instructed in developing music skills when they were children. Thus they become unwitting participants in an unfortunate cycle.

Parents need not be amateur or professional musicians to guide and to instruct their children in developing music skills, just as they need not be professional writers, speakers, or mathematicians to teach their children how to communicate with the spoken and written word, or how to deal with workaday arithmetic. Parents who simply sing with relatively good intonation and move their bodies with flexible and free flowing movement, even though they may not play a music instrument, meet the basic requirements for guiding and instructing their children in developing music skills. Unless parents rise to that responsibility, either by themselves or with the assistance of teachers and friends, their children will be limited throughout their lives in their ability to understand and to appreciate music. In time children will assume that life and art are poles apart, because they will have forgotten that art is life and that life is art.

Music is unique to humans. Like the other arts, music is as basic as language to human development and existence. Through music a child gains insights into herself, into others, and into life itself. Perhaps most important, she is better able to develop and sustain her imagination. Without music, life would be bleak. Because a day does not pass without a child's hearing or participating in some music, it is to a child's advantage to understand music as thoroughly as she can. As a result, as she becomes older she will learn to appreciate, to listen to, and to partake

2

in music that she herself believes to be good. Because of such cultural awareness, her life will have more meaning for her.

The purpose of this book is to help parents, preschool teachers, and music teachers to recognize the importance of early childhood music, to discover how very young children learn music, to provide opportunities for guiding very young children to learn for and from themselves, and to determine how very young children might best be taught music. The intent is not to prepare young children to be professional musicians or to identify and foster musical geniuses. Rather, it is to explain to parents and to teachers how they might informally guide young children to an understanding of music just as they have informally guided them to an understanding of their spoken language before they received formal schooling. Nothing should be demanded or expected of young children in terms of their musical responses. It must be remembered that, like speech development, a child's music development is not immediate. Moreover, in our society it is common for evidence of a child's music development to present itself later than evidence of her speech development. It also must be remembered that to delay a child's transition from informal guidance to formal instruction in music may be almost as detrimental as to neglect giving her any informal guidance in music at all.

Preschool child•en must not be taught as if they are young adults or kindergarten children; nor should the assessment and the development of their musical capabilities be based upon comparisons with what adults can or cannot do. Young children learn as much, and possibly more, from themselves and one another as they learn from adults. Nonetheless, if adults take the necessary time to give proper attention to the music development of young children, and if the children's comprehension is not underestimated by the adult who is guiding them, young children will become comfortable with all types of music at an early age, and positive attitudes toward music will persist throughout their lives. Equally important, when they become adults, they will be more appreciative audiences. They may even read a music score as easily as they read a book. Should music become a profession rather than an avocation for a child, that should be considered an unexpected benefit.

Consider how a young child learns a language. As a newborn, she hears language being spoken all around her. Ideally, the young child is read to even before she can understand language. She absorbs what she

3

hears. Soon she begins to make speech sounds. In her language babble she experiments with sounds that may be found in a number of languages. By the age of eight months the child at least has acquired the readiness to articulate the necessary sounds with her tongue to speak the language of her culture. Adults and siblings speak to her on a one to one basis, and they offer her informal guidance in forming words. Soon the young child "breaks the code" of the language of her culture and begins to imitate words. In using those words, she begins to create her own phrases and sentences as she communicates with others. Later she begins to read and write words and sentences that she has heard and spoken. The whole process, with the possible exception of reading and writing, takes place before a child enters kindergarten or first grade. Unless such a process, which depends upon structured and unstructured informal guidance, occurs before a child enters kindergarten or first grade, the child will not have the necessary readiness to profit from formal language instruction. For a child to be successful in school, she must enter kindergarten or first grade with at least a listening and a speaking vocabulary. After she has developed rich listening and speaking vocabularies, it will be to her advantage, additionally, to be informally guided in developing rudimentary reading and writing vocabularies at home before being given formal language instruction in school.

Although music is a literature and not a language, children learn music in much the same way that they learn a language. Unfortunately, most children are not given unstructured or structured guidance at home to encourage them to engage in music babble and to learn music. Such guidance that is needed and should be similar to that which is given to encourage them to engage in language babble and to learn their language.

There are at least two stages to music babble. One is a tonal babble stage and the other is a rhythm babble stage. Though there are probably more, other music babble stages have not yet been objectively identified. A child may emerge from tonal babble and rhythm babble at the same time or from one before the other. The sooner a child emerges from a music babble stage, the more musical she may be expected to be throughout her life.

When in the tonal babble stage, a child attempts to sing with a speaking voice quality. The relationships among the sounds that she makes have little or nothing in common with the music of her culture. When in the rhythm babble stage, the child's sounds and movements are erratic. They are not in a consistent tempo, and they lack continuity in terms of the meters of her culture. Through an adult typically cannot make sense of a child's music babble, it is possible that a child may understand her own babble and that of other children.

The typically newborn is sung to much less than she is spoken to. Moreover, she hears music performed much less than she hears language spoken. When she does hear music, it usually happens more as a matter of chance than of intent. As a result, she does not have the opportunity to absorb the sound of music as she does the sound of language, and her ability to move through music babble is hindered. Thus the young child is unable to leave the tonal and rhythm babble stages to develop basic listening vocabularies in music. Without such listening vocabularies to serve as readinesses for her further music development, she becomes restricted in, if not prevented from, acquiring a "speaking" vocabulary in music. The speaking vocabulary in music is the ability to move the body with flexible and flowing movement, to breathe freely, to sing tonal patterns, and to chant rhythm patterns. Without having developed listening and speaking vocabularies in music, a child will not be able to understand and relate to the music of her culture.

To develop the necessary readiness to learn music when she is older, the child must have experienced a rich and varied exposure to music before she is eighteen months old. By the time a child is eighteen months old she becomes preoccupied with language acquisition, and music is of secondary importance to her. Even with a rich and varied exposure to music, the rhythm of a child's spoken language will significantly affect the way her tongue moves when she performs music, and particularly the way she artistically and stylistically expresses music.

Although a typical young child hears music haphazardly through the media, and may even hear live music, rarely does an adult attempt to teach her to use her singing voice as she teaches her to use her speaking voice. Just as all children can learn to use their speaking voices, so all children can learn to use their singing voices. Whether they learn to speak intelligently and learn to sing musically depends upon structured and unstructured informal guidance and formal instruction in interaction with music aptitude. Moreover, rarely does an adult sing tonal patterns and chant rhythm patterns to or with a young child. Songs or lullabies may be sung to her, but she is expected neither to participate (babble) nor to learn to sing tonal patterns and to chant rhythm patterns with the accuracy with which she learns to speak words in language. Therefore, the typical young child does not acquire the listening vocabulary needed to develop singing and chanting vocabularies. And for those children who do, an adult usually does not systematically spend time in helping them to develop those vocabularies. The lack of adult intervention may sometimes be a blessing, however, because an overzealous adult may unwittingly encourage or even demand the premature performance of a song from the child. To expect a child to learn to sing a song, with or without the text, without her first being able to sing tonal patterns and chant rhythm patterns, is like expecting her to recite poems before she can speak individual words, phrases, and sentences.

That most young children are not given adequate opportunity to develop a listening vocabulary in music stands in the way of their music development. Optimally, the young child's singing and chanting vocabularies should develop as a result of the interaction of those two vocabularies with her tonal and rhythm listening vocabularies, and her tonal and rhythm listening vocabularies should develop as a result of the interaction of those two vocabularies with her singing and chanting vocabularies. It is a continuous developmental cycle. The tonal and rhythm listening vocabularies on the one hand and the singing and chanting vocabularies on the other become interdependent as the young child learns music. Moreover, if a child is not encouraged to move continuously with flexibility in free flowing movement, she will learn to chant rhythm patterns with rigidity, if indeed she develops a chanting vocabulary at all. Too often the young child is not encouraged to babble tonal patterns and rhythm patterns, nor is she later encouraged to perform tonal patterns and rhythm patterns by herself with a degree of accuracy similar to that expected of her when she is learning to pronounce words. Possibly because the body itself knows before the brain comprehends, children begin to teach themselves flexible and free flowing movement and rhythm at a very early age. Unfortunately, for whatever reason or reasons most likely related to adult intervention, most of them do not persist in those endeavors. Without proper informal guidance in music, they are limited in their ability to learn to move with flexible and free flowing movement at about the time they begin formal music instruction. Children who have been deprived of appropriate early music development will be able only to learn about music when they begin to receive formal music instruction in school. There is little doubt that they will find it difficult to learn to perform musically.

If a child who has not received structured and unstructured informal guidance in music before she enters school is given formal instruction in music in kindergarten and first grade, difficulties are created and compounded as a result of the way music is taught in many schools. For example, in order to develop language skills in school, it is understood that a child will continue to engage in individual speaking. In contrast, many music teachers do not think it is necessary or wise to teach all children to perform individually, or even to offer them the opportunity to perform individually. The child usually sings only in groups. Imagine the outcome in terms of language learning if a child were asked to speak only in groups. She would learn only to imitate what others around her were saying, and she would not give meaning to what was being said. She might never create a sentence of her own or express her own thoughts. It is no wonder that with such music instruction many children cannot develop an understanding of music. As a result, they are simply dismissed as being "untalented" by their teachers and parents.

When a child enters kindergarten or first grade, she receives instruction in language for a substantial part of every school day. Thus a teacher may be held accountable for a child's language development in accordance with an established curriculum; records are kept, measurement procedures precede evaluation procedures, and both become standard practice. In contrast, a child typically receives instruction in music once or possibly twice a week for a period of 20 to 45 minutes. Because there is inadequate time devoted to formal music instruction, and because there is no generally accepted sequential curriculum in music, the music skills that a child is expected to have in the second grade that she did not have in the first grade, for example, are not given consideration. At most, only subjective evaluation which cannot be based upon objective measurement is possible. Entertainment and recreation with some explanation of notation seem to be the mainstay of most programs in formal music instruction. If the children are having "fun," it is assumed that the music program is successful. It must be remembered, however, that children can experience just as much fun, and usually more, when they are engaging in more worthwhile music activities. Whereas fun is temporary, an understanding of music sustains one throughout life.

Adults in a society instill in their young what they consider to be of value. Adults who have not developed music skills and who, at best, were not taught music but only about music, are not in a position to place the value on music that it deserves. Parents tend to teach their children as they as children were taught and what they as adults like and seemingly understand. If it is true that the state of a society is reflected in whom it chooses as its heroes, it is obvious that music in the United States is not held in very high esteem. Such circumstances are not easily changed. It takes time and education, not scolding and preaching, for a society to understand that it must put the same value on music that it does, for example, on sports and literature, and much more than it does on standard television fare. A course in music appreciation, remedial or otherwise, no longer serves even as a "quick fix." The remainder of this book is dedicated to bringing about a change in music education. That goal is possible to achieve. After all, the majority of persons living 250 years ago could not even read words, and certainly could not read with comprehension the language that they spoke.

Chapter Two

MUSIC APTITUDES

To understand how young children learn music and how they are best taught music, it is necessary to understand the role of music aptitude in the learning and teaching of music. Music aptitude is different from music achievement. Music aptitude is a child's potential to learn music; it represents "inner possibilities." Music achievement is what a child has learned relative to his music aptitude; it represents "outer actuality."

The primary purpose of measuring children's music aptitudes is to enable a teacher to adapt music instruction to each child's individual musical needs, whether those children are taught in groups or privately. Whereas a young child's music aptitude can be measured objectively through the use of a valid test, his music achievement is best measured subjectively through controlled and systematic observation. The measurement of music aptitude and music achievement can take place in either the preschool or the home. Because the home is more familiar to the young child, more valid results are derived when assessment is undertaken in the home. A teacher may evaluate a young child's singing and chanting in preschool or by listening to a recording of him performing informally and spontaneously in his home.

Every child is born with some music aptitude. Like many other traits, music aptitude is normally distributed among children at birth. That means that approximately 68 percent are born with average music aptitude, approximately 16 percent with above average music aptitude, and approximately 16 percent with below average music aptitude. Just as there are no children without intelligence, so there are no children without music aptitude.

A child's music aptitude is innate, but it is affected by his environment. Because the music environment for only a few newborns is appropriate and as rich as it should be, it is reasoned that the level of music aptitude with which a child is born begins to decrease shortly after birth. A child's music aptitude continues to decrease until his music environment becomes appropriate. When the music environment becomes appropriate, a child's music aptitude will begin to increase toward its birth level. Regardless of how positive the quality of the music environment becomes, however, a child's music aptitude will never rise above its birth level. For a variety of reasons, the music aptitudes of most, if not all, children never again reach, though they may approach, birth levels.

It has been speculated that the level of music aptitude with which a child is born, his innate potential, may be to some extent a result of his prenatal responsiveness to music as well as to the quality of the music environment that his mother experienced during her pregnancy. It can be understood why some cultures consider a child to be approximately a year old at the time of his birth.

The sooner a child begins to enjoy a rich music environment, the sooner his music aptitude will begin to move upward toward its initial level, and the closer it will come to reaching and stabilizing at that level. For example, consider two children born with the same level of music aptitude. The child who experiences a rich music environment at six months of age will ultimately demonstrate a higher level of music aptitude than the child who experiences a similarly rich music environment at eighteen months of age. The effect of a rich music environment on a child's music aptitude decreases at an increasing rate as the child grows older. The importance of an early and rich music environment cannot be overestimated. By the time a child reaches approximately age nine, his level of music aptitude is no longer affected by his music environment, even by a music environment of extremely high quality.

Because the music aptitude of a child who is younger than nine years of age is a product of both innate potential and early music environmental influences, music aptitude that is measured during the first nine years of life is called developmental music aptitude. Because music environmental influences have no effect on a child's music aptitude after he is nine years old, music aptitude that is measured after that time is called stabilized music aptitude. The basis of both developmental music aptitude and stabilized music aptitude is called audiation. Whether a child is in or has emerged from the music babble stage, he is able to engage to at least some extent in audiation.

Audiation, which is further described in forthcoming chapters and is explained in detail elsewhere (Gordon, 1989), takes place when one "hears" *and comprehends* music for which the sound is no longer or never has been physically present. For example, pretend that you are hearing a group of children sing "Happy Birthday." If you can do that with some degree of musical precision and if you can understand some of the musical characteristics of the song, such as its tonality and meter, to some extent you are audiating the song. Audiation is to music as thinking is to language. Audiating while performing is like thinking while speaking.

The degree to which a child can audiate two tonal patterns as being the same as each other or different from each other and the degree to which he can audiate two rhythm patterns as being the same as each other or different from each other are measures of his tonal and rhythm aptitudes. Just as it may be assumed that the more words that a child can think with, the higher is his IQ (intellectual aptitude), it may also be assumed that the more tonal patterns and rhythm patterns that a child can audiate, the higher is his music aptitude. If a child is consistent in identifying those pairs of tonal patterns that sound different and in identifying those pairs of rhythm patterns that sound different, he is considered to have high developmental tonal aptitude and high developmental rhythm aptitude. A child with low developmental music aptitude finds it easier to audiate correctly a pair of tonal patterns or a pair of rhythm patterns that sound the same than to audiate correctly a pair of tonal patterns or a pair of rhythm patterns that sound different. On the other hand, regardless of level of developmental music aptitudes, and in terms of music achievement, it is easier for children to perform a pair of tonal patterns or a pair of rhythm patterns that are different than to perform a pair of tonal patterns or a pair of rhythm patterns that are the same.

It is rare for a child to have a very high tonal aptitude and a very high rhythm aptitude, or to have a very low tonal aptitude and a very low rhythm aptitude. It is not unusual for a child to have an average tonal aptitude and an average rhythm aptitude. Nonetheless, in a given group of children, even in a restricted chronological age range, the difference between each child's tonal aptitude score and his rhythm aptitude score is usually much greater than the difference between the mean tonal aptitude score and the mean rhythm aptitude score for the group of which he is a member.

Two similarities between developmental music aptitude and stabilized music aptitude are, first, that both types of music aptitudes are distributed among persons in such a way that some demonstrate low

11

levels, the majority demonstrate average levels, and some demonstrate high levels, and second, that both types of music aptitudes are based upon audiation. The differences between the two types of music aptitudes, however, are more significant than the similarities. First, stabilized music aptitude includes more dimensions than does developmental music aptitude. Whereas more than two dozen stabilized music aptitudes have been identified, there are only two known developmental music aptitudes. Melody, harmony, tempo, meter, phrasing, balance, and style are the seven most important stabilized music aptitudes. Tonal and rhythm are the two developmental music aptitudes. Second, children in the developmental music aptitude stage are not able to attend to either the tonal dimension of music or the rhythm dimension of music when the two dimensions are heard at the same time. Third, children in the developmental music aptitude stage are not able to show reliable preferences as to which of two music phrases sounds better than the other. Children younger than age nine are more interested in how music is constructed than they are in the expressive qualities of music. It is possible, however, that an harmonic as well as an aesthetic aptitude is latent in young children. Fourth, children in the developmental music aptitude stage are not able to perceive differences reliably in dynamics and timbres unless those differences are extreme. One tonal pattern or rhythm pattern must be very loud and the other very soft, and one tonal pattern or one rhythm pattern must have a very rich timbre and the other a very sterile timbre before children are able to audiate dynamic and timbre differences.

As explained, young children go through a music babble stage just as they go through a language babble stage. If a child is not given structured and unstructured informal guidance in music development as he passes through the tonal and rhythm babble stages, guidance as rich as the structured and unstructured informal guidance given him when he passes through the language babble stage, one or both of his music aptitudes will not develop to as high a level as they might have with the benefit of such guidance.

A young child requires assistance in learning to decode the music of his culture just as he requires assistance in learning to decode the language of his culture. Because a nine year old child's level of developmental music aptitude becomes his stabilized level of music aptitude, a lack of structured and unstructured informal guidance directed at helping the child decode the music of his culture, thus helping him to work through the music babble stage, will affect his later music achievement.

Music babble is most commonly associated with young children, but older children, and even some adults, sometimes are still in either the tonal babble stage or the rhythm babble stage, or both. Such extended music babble stages occur when an adult was not given structured and unstructured informal guidance in music in childhood and now lacks the motivation and a high enough level of stabilized music aptitude to enable him to work his way out of music babble without assistance. Therefore, although music babble is characteristic of a child who is in the developmental music aptitude stage, and ideally occurs within the first half of the nine years during which a child is in the developmental music aptitude stage, music babble also may be associated with a child who is in the stabilized music aptitude stage. Regardless of how low a child's innate potential is, with proper structured and unstructured informal guidance in music he is capable of emerging from music babble. The older the child is, however, the more difficult it will be for him to emerge from music babble. Extra-musical factors, particularly personality traits, often prevent older children and adults, even those with high stabilized music aptitudes, from progressing beyond music babble. When a child becomes an adult, the chances of his leaving the music babble stage, regardless of how high the level of his stabilized music aptitude, are greatly reduced.

It is possible for a child with high developmental music aptitude to remain in the tonal and rhythm music babble stages after a child of the same age with low developmental music aptitude has left those stages. Children with high developmental music aptitude who are given structured and unstructured informal guidance in music typically emerge from a music babble stage sooner than do children with low developmental music aptitude who are also given structured and unstructured informal guidance in music. The purpose of structured and unstructured informal guidance in music is not to force a child to emerge from a music babble stage before he is psychologically and physically ready to do so. If a child emerges from a music babble stage prematurely, it is possible that his music achievement will be impaired as he becomes older. That is especially the case for a child with high developmental music aptitude who emerges from a music babble stage without first having had structured and unstructured informal guidance in music. Many children begin to learn to play an instrument without having had such guidance. In such a case a child's attainment of long range music development is sacrificed to his attainment of a short range goal.

When a child takes himself out of a music babble stage without the benefit of structured and unstructured informal guidance from a knowledgeable and concerned adult, it can be expected that he will lack the necessary foundation to engage in and profit fully from formal music instruction. Moreover, emotional as well as physical problems may accompany the musical frustration that the child will encounter, particularly if the study of an instrument is begun prematurely. Under no circumstances should an emotionally immature child be rushed out of a music babble stage. The comfort through security that a child finds in music babble will prove to be beneficial to him when he is naturally ready to leave music babble. Children with high developmental music aptitude, even those who are more emotionally and physically mature, can be truly considered disadvantaged or disabled if they are forced to try to leave a music babble stage before they have the proper music readiness to do so. Only with appropriate structured and unstructured informal guidance in music can a child safely emerge from music babble.

There are two types of music aptitude tests: developmental and stabilized. The *Musical Aptitude Profile* (Gordon, 1988, 1965) is a test of stabilized music aptitude. It is designed for students in elementary school through high school. The *Advanced Measures of Music Audiation* (Gordon, 1989) is also a stabilized music aptitude test. It is designed for college students. The *Intermediate Measures of Music Audiation* (Gordon, 1982) is a test of developmental music aptitude. It is designed for children six to eleven years old. The *Primary Measures of Music Audiation* (Gordon, 1979) is also a test of developmental music aptitude. It is designed for children five to eight years old. *Audie* (Gordon, 1989), another test of developmental music aptitude, is designed for children three and four years old. All of the tests are recorded. Also, all of the tests except *Audie* are group tests. They can be administered to many students at the same time. Audie is designed to be individually administered by a parent at home or by a teacher in school.

Either the *Musical Aptitude Profile* or the *Intermediate Measures of Music Audiation* may be used with nine, ten, and eleven year old children. The former serves more diagnostic functions than the latter. When fifty percent of the children to whom the *Primary Measures of Music Audiation* is administered score above the eightieth percentile on the *Tonal* test, the *Rhythm* test, or both, the *Intermediate Measures of Music Audiation*, which is like the *Primary Measures of Music Audiation* except that it includes more complex content, should be administered to those children.

There are various purposes for using a music aptitude test. The most important one is for the improvement of guidance and instruction in music. A valid music aptitude test can be used to diagnose a child's musical strengths and weaknesses without comparing his scores with those of other children. That is an idiographic assessment. A valid music aptitude test can be used also to describe the individual musical differences among children by comparing one child's scores with those of other children. That is a normative assessment.

With regard to the idiographic assessment, when a parent or teacher knows, for example, that a child has a high tonal aptitude and a low rhythm aptitude, provision can be made in guidance and instruction for compensating for the child's low rhythm aptitude while at the same time enhancing his high tonal aptitude. To treat the child as if he had average overall music aptitude would be to do his musical development harm. When a child is in the developmental music aptitude stage, attention must be given to attempting to raise the lower of his two developmental music aptitude scores. The sooner the child's deficiency is dealt with, the sooner and the higher the developmental aptitude score in question may rise. How guidance and instruction in music are adapted to children's individual musical differences as shown by their music aptitude test scores is explained in later chapters.

With regard to the normative assessment, although a child's rhythm aptitude score may be higher than his tonal aptitude score, the former may be, for example, at only the 40th percentile. How a child's rhythm aptitude should be dealt with if it is, for example, at the 40th percentile is different from how it should be dealt with if it is at the 90th percentile. Perhaps the least important purpose of a music aptitude test is the one for which it is most frequently used: to identify those children with the highest overall music aptitude who are most likely to succeed in special music instruction. The parents of such children are usually incorrectly advised to have their children take lessons on a music instrument, regardless of the status of the child's music babble, his emotional readiness, or his need to have his lower music aptitude given immediate special attention without the distraction of instrumental instruction.

It must be assumed that a child with high music achievement has high music aptitude. It may not be assumed that a child with low music achievement, one who does not sing, for example, has low music aptitude. Many children who have relatively high music aptitude have relatively low music achievement, because they have not received structured and unstructured informal guidance in music. They have not been given the opportunity to learn music to the extent that their music aptitude will allow. Without the use of a valid music aptitude test, those children might go through life without anyone's ever suspecting that they have or had the potential to achieve high standards in music, avocationally or vocationally. Approximately half of the children with overall music aptitude in the upper twenty percent who attend public and private schools are never identified by the music faculty, and they never receive special guidance or instruction in music. It is difficult to understand how such a waste of human potential can take place.

All humans excel in some ways and not in others. They tend to use their strengths to compensate for their weaknesses. Children with high overall music aptitude are typically found to be deficient in other aptitudes, and children with low overall music aptitude are typically found to excel in other aptitudes. That is particularly the case with regard to music aptitude and IQ. There is virtually no relationship between music aptitude and academic intelligence. Some children with high music aptitude have high academic intelligence and others have average or low academic intelligence. Similarly, some children with high academic intelligence have high music aptitude and others have average or low music aptitude. Although the relationship between music aptitude and academic achievement is somewhat higher than that between music aptitude and academic intelligence, neither academic achievement nor academic intelligence tests, nor any other type of test, should be used as a substitute for a music aptitude test.

A music aptitude test should be used to reveal a child's music aptitude. Without the use of such a test, a child's music aptitude may be forever concealed. Every child, regardless of his level of music aptitude, can profit from structured and unstructured informal guidance and formal instruction in music. A child should never be labeled or denied guidance or instruction in music because of his music aptitude test scores. Such misuse of a music aptitude test is worse than not using a test at all. When used with judgment and wisdom to adapt music instruction to the individual musical needs of every child, the results of a valid music

16

aptitude test can assist in preventing children from experiencing psychological problems that arise when they are taught as if all of them have average music aptitude. When guidance and instruction in music are undertaken without knowledge of their music aptitudes, it is not uncommon for children with low music aptitude to become frustrated and children with high music aptitude to become bored. A detailed explanation and discussion of the nature and development of music aptitude and of music aptitude tests may be found elsewhere (Gordon, 1986).

Chapter Three

AUDIATION AND MUSIC LEARNING THEORY

Audiation

Audiation takes place when one hears *and comprehends* music silently, when the sound of music is no longer or never has been physically present. In contrast, aural perception takes place when one hears music of which the sound is physically present. As will be explained, it is possible for one to hear, recognize, imitate, and memorize music without being able to audiate that music.

Audiation is the basis of music aptitude. The extent to which a child *intuitively* audiates elemental sound in music and organizes that sound in any way that she desires is a measure of her music aptitude. The level of developmental music aptitude or stabilized music aptitude that a child demonstrates is an indication of her potential for learning how to audiate in a culturally accepted and more complex manner than her mere intuition will allow. Audiation is also the medium through which a child learns to achieve in music. It is through structured and unstructured informal guidance in music that a child uses her *intuition* and better learns *how* to audiate *cognitively*. It is through formal instruction in music that a child continues to learn to audiate cognitively and, in addition, learns *what* to audiate. A child cannot be taught the potential to audiate. That is a matter of music aptitude. Just as the potential to think is a birthright, so is the potential to audiate a birthright. A child, however, can be taught how to develop her audiation potential and be taught what to audiate. That is a matter of music achievement.

Audiation is not acquired immediately or quickly. Skill in audiation is acquired through a sequential process over time. Unless one can audiate a piece of music, she will not truly understand and will probably lose interest in and forget that piece of music.

There are various types of audiation. Children may audiate while listening to music, recalling music, performing music (through singing, moving, or playing an instrument), or creating music. Older children may audiate when they read and write music. It may seem contradictory that a child can hear music and at the same time audiate that music. The fact is that as she hears music, she is perceiving only the sound of that music

18

the moment that it is heard. It is not until a moment or so after hearing the music that the child audiates (silently gives meaning to) what she has heard as she perceives and then sequentially audiates the additional sounds that follow in the music. As the child audiates, she may be anticipating what she will be hearing next in the music, whether the music is familiar or not.

Though music and language are different, the process of audiating while listening to music is like the process of thinking while listening to language. There is language and there is thought. There is music and there is audiation. Just as language and thought have different roots and develop differently, so music and audiation have different roots and develop differently. Language and music have a biological basis, whereas thought and audiation have a psychological basis.

There are seven types of audiation and six stages of audiation. The seven types of audiation take place as one is 1) listening to familiar or unfamiliar music, 2) reading silently, vocally, or instrumentally the notation of familiar or unfamiliar music, 3) notating familiar or unfamiliar music from dictation, 4) recalling familiar music silently, vocally, or instrumentally, 5) notating familiar music from recall, 6) creating or improvising unfamiliar music silently, vocally, or instrumentally, and 7) notating unfamiliar music that one has created or improvised. The six stages of audiation, which are hierarchical, cyclic, and cumulative, presumably take place in the following sequence as one is listening to music: 1) sound is heard and retained, 2) that sound is organized in audiation into a series of tonal patterns and rhythm patterns, 3) music syntax, the tonality and meter which form the foundation for those tonal patterns and rhythm patterns, is audiated, 4) the tonal patterns and rhythm patterns that have already been organized in the music which is being heard are held in audiation, 5) tonal patterns and rhythm patterns that have been audiated in other pieces of music, which are significantly similar to or different from those that are being held in audiation from the music currently being heard, are recalled and compared in audiation, and 6) predictions are made in audiation about the tonal patterns and rhythm patterns that will be heard next in the music.

Audiation is often confused with aural imagery as well as with aural perception. When a child aurally perceives, she is hearing music of which the sound is physically present. Aural perception is an obvious prerequisite to audiation. Unless a child is capable of aurally perceiving the sound of music that is physically present, she will be incapable of audiating music. The term "imagery" is properly associated with the visual sense, not the aural sense. Thus the term "aural imagery" is a contradiction that leads to confusion, unless perhaps it is meant to signify the audiation of what is seen in notation. In that case, the term "notational audiation" is more appropriate, and further, that term makes clear the distinction between audiation and notational audiation. It is important to understand that one is able to audiate without having any knowledge of notation or music theory.

Audiation is confused also with inner hearing, imitation, recognition, and memorization. Inner hearing and imitation contribute to the same type of response to music. A child can imitate or "inner hear" without audiating. As it is possible for a child to learn to utter nonsense syllables, such as "ah ga bah," or to repeat a passage in a foreign language without knowing the meaning of what she is saying, so a child can learn to sing a song by rote without giving it musical meaning, that is, without understanding the musical organization and structure of the song. The child is imitating but not audiating. It is even possible for a child to repeat so quickly what an adult or another child beside her is singing that it is not apparent that she is imitating the adult or the other child and that she is not audiating. That such a child's skill in imitating is highly developed, and that it is developed to a much greater extent than is her audiation skill, become obvious when she is asked to sing alone and unaccompanied. It is common to discover that although a group of children can perform a song in ensemble relatively free of errors, only one or two children in the group may be able to sing the song in solo with good intonation and rhythm. Those few children are audiating, whereas the majority of the children are only imitating as they rely heavily on the words of the song.

Although audiation and imitation are different, they are not mutually exclusive. The ability to imitate is a necessary readiness for learning how to audiate. A child may be able to imitate without being able to audiate, but she will not be able to audiate unless she is first able to imitate. Children in the developmental music aptitude stage, who are either in or out of music babble, emphasize imitation over audiation. It is possible that the ability to imitate music may be more related to IQ than to music aptitude. Children in the stabilized music aptitude stage who have been appropriately guided out of music babble emphasize audiation over imitation.

Imitation is accomplished through someone else's ears. Audiation is accomplished through one's own ears. Imitating while singing a song is analogous to using tracing paper to copy a picture. Audiating while singing a song is analogous to visualizing and then drawing a picture. A child imitates when she repeats what she heard just a fraction of a second or a few seconds before. What is imitated is soon forgotten. A child audiates when she retains and understands what she heard seconds, minutes, hours, days, weeks, months, or even years before. What is audiated is rarely forgotten. What is audiated can be recalled by associating characteristics of the music with specific musical meaning.

Audiation is a process which engenders musical understanding. Imitation, by itself, does not. Imitation deals with parts of the whole. Audiation deals with the whole. Nonetheless, the importance of imitation is not diminished by its distinction from audiation. Unless a child first learns to imitate, she will not be able to learn to audiate, either through structured or unstructured informal guidance or formal instruction in music. Although audiation requires more complex processes than imitation, it is based upon imitation.

To perform music as a musician, that is, with good intonation, good rhythm, and sensitive expression, one must audiate the music that is being performed so that it can be interpreted. To audiate while performing music is like thinking while speaking. It is clear that a child who is taking lessons on an instrument but cannot audiate is at a disadvantage. Consider jazz musicians. Unless they can audiate, they cannot improvise. It is through the audiation of chord progressions and meter and the anticipation of forthcoming parts of a familiar song that a soloist is able to improvise an appropriate variation of the original melody of that song.

There is also a difference between recognizing music and audiating music. Imitation is the readiness for learning how to audiate, whereas recognition is the readiness for learning how to imitate. One may be able to recognize a piece of music when it is heard, but not be able to audiate it or perform it from recall either vocally or instrumentally. On the other hand, if one can audiate a piece of music, she will, of course, recognize it when it is heard. Although the recognition of a piece of music requires less understanding of music than the audiation of a piece of music, children and adults recognize the

21

timbres of different speaking voices more readily than they do the sounds of different singing voices.

One may recognize, for example, the difference between good and bad intonation in a piece of music but may not be able to perform that piece of music vocally or instrumentally with good intonation. One cannot perform with better intonation and rhythm than she can audiate. The ability to audiate as well as to recognize various musical aspects of a piece of music is indicative of music understanding, and thus generally of music appreciation.

Music is not a language, because it does not have a grammar or parts of speech. Music does have syntax, however, because there is logical order in its sounds. Meaning is given to music through syntax. To comprehend syntax in a piece of music, one must audiate its organization and structure. If, while listening to, performing, reading, improvising, or creating music a child is simultaneously and continuously audiating the tonality (for example, major or harmonic minor) and the meter (for example, duple or triple) of the music, she is then audiating the syntax of the music. To comprehend the elemental syntax of a piece of music, a child must be concurrently audiating at least five aspects of the music: pitches moving in different directions, the resting tone of the music, different durations moving ahead, the placement of macro beats in the music, and the tempo of the music. A child who is capable of such audiation has, of course, at the very least emerged from both tonal and rhythm babble.

The syntax of music can be audiated also in terms of form, style, harmony, modulations, dynamics, and timbre. Without audiation there can be no sequence, repetition, and contrast in music, and without those factors there can be no form in music. The only way that one can know when a piece of music is coming to an end, for example, is through audiation. Unless she is audiating, a listener may be tempted to applaud at any time during a performance. The more ways in which a listener is able to audiate syntax in music, the better able she is to understand music and, of course, the higher is her overall music aptitude. The greater then should be her music achievement and appreciation.

Musical memory and the memorization of music are different. Through musical memory one is able to remember in audiation what she has heard performed, to anticipate in audiation what she will hear performed, and then to coordinate information from those two dimensions of audiation (recall and prediction) with what she is hearing performed. Musical memory and audiation are linked, because musical memory allows audiation to take place and to flourish, and audiation stimulates musical memory. Without audiation to sustain it, musical memory becomes memorization. The emphasis in memorization is on what is to be performed next, regardless of whether it makes musical sense or not. In contrast to musical memory, which deals with the audiation of tonal patterns and rhythm patterns as they interact with tonality and meter, memorization is a mechanical process which deals only with individual notes and/or fingerings. Just as it is possible for one to memorize and to recite a poem without being able to explain its meaning, so it is possible for one to memorize and to perform a piece of music without being able to audiate it, that is, without being able to comprehend the organization and structure of the music.

While performing a piece of music on an instrument, a child may make a mistake. The child who is audiating is able to correct the mistake by making an appropriate adjustment (as in intonation), and she is secure enough in her audiation not to be distracted by the mistake. The child who has memorized a piece of music and is not audiating is unable to cope with the mistake. When she makes a mistake, her typical reaction is to stop, then to try to visualize the notation of the music or to practice some fingerings or muscular movement, and then to begin performing the music again from the beginning. For the child who has memorized, there are "wrong" notes. For the child who is audiating, there are appropriate solutions.

It is unfortunate that many students are taught to perform music that they have memorized rather than being taught how to use their musical memories to audiate and to give meaning to that music. Many of them may never learn to audiate what they perform. Particularly when learning to play music instruments, many children are told to listen to the teacher perform a piece of music and to "play it that way." Fingerings and motor skills become the compelling factors. In such cases a child is being taught by rote to imitate and to memorize on her instrument what she hears her teacher perform. She is not being taught to audiate what she is learning to perform. The child's instrumental performance may be technically acceptable, but it will prove to be musically dull. The reason is that it is not possible for a performer to assess critically what she is hearing herself play if she cannot audiate beforehand what she intends to play. Her inept performance will lack sensitivity and expression, because she has been trained rather than taught.

Results are similar when a child is taught to perform on a music instrument by reading notation in association with the memorization of fingerings before she can audiate the music that she sees in notation, that is, before she can notationally audiate. The child is told to read and to memorize the music so that she can perform it without actually seeing the notation, although she may be encouraged to visualize the notation. Memorization through the visualization of notation and memorization through imitating "by ear" lead to the same unsatisfactory results in instrumental performance. When she learns through imitation and memorization, a child becomes totally dependent upon someone else. At best, music will have only extrinsic meaning for her; she will learn only about the music. When she learns through audiation, a child develops the necessary skill and self-confidence to comprehend the syntax of the music. Music will have intrinsic meaning for her; she will learn the music itself.

Without a breath during which an instrumentalist audiates what is to be performed before she performs it, she builds tension in her performance. It is as a result of audiation that the instrumentalist is able to take in adequate breath, neither too little nor too much, to perform the one or more phrases that she is audiating. Most technical errors in instrumental performance arise as a result of the performer's not audiating what she intends to perform.

When there is agreement that a piece of music is in a given tonality, that music is said to have objective tonality. When there is not agreement that a piece of music is in a specific tonality, that music is said to have subjective tonality. The same is true for meter. Whether a child is audiating objective or subjective tonality or objective or subjective meter in a piece of music, the fact that she is audiating a tonality and a meter at all, means that she is giving syntax to the music. Children still in music babble are able to give only subjective tonality and subjective meter to music. That is, they are able to learn to communicate with themselves. Children who have emerged from music babble are able to give objective tonality and objective meter to music. That is, they are able to learn to communicate with others. As a result of such objectivity, they are also able to learn to give appropriate subjective tonality and subjective meter to contemporary music. Given structured and unstructured informal

24

guidance in music while they are in music babble, children in the developmental music aptitude stage will be able to learn both to imitate and to audiate with subjective tonality and subjective meter before they leave music babble. Once they have emerged from music babble, whether they are in the developmental music aptitude stage or the stabilized music aptitude stage, children who received structured and unstructured informal guidance in music when they were in music babble will be better able to learn to audiate with objective tonality and objective meter.

Music Learning Theory

Appropriate music learning theory forms the foundation for appropriate learning sequence activities. Music learning theory is the explanation of how children learn music. Learning sequence activities are the practical application of the principles of music learning theory. Thus music learning theory and learning sequence activities, depending upon the context within which they are being discussed, are terms that are used interchangeably throughout this book.

The types and stages of audiation are closely allied with music learning theory. How audiation and music learning theory interact when students are given formal instruction in music is explained elsewhere (Gordon, 1989). The following summary of that information is intended to provide the reader with the necessary background for understanding the next four chapters. In those chapters is an explanation of the relationship between preparatory audiation and music learning theory that takes place with structured and unstructured informal guidance in music. Whereas the types and stages of *audiation* and the levels of music learning theory have independent roles in formal instruction in music, the types and stages of *preparatory audiation* and music learning theory are one and the same in structured and unstructured informal guidance in music.

With regard to formal instruction in music, there are three music learning theories. The first is called skill learning sequence; the second, tonal content learning sequence; and the third, rhythm content learning sequence. Only skill learning sequence need be summarized at this time. Tonal content learning sequence and rhythm content learning sequence, along with skill learning sequence, are alluded to in Chapter Nine.

25

As seen in the outline on the following page, skill learning sequence has two parts: discrimination learning and inference learning. Discrimination learning is rote learning. Inference learning is a matter of making judgments and drawing conclusions based upon knowledge that was acquired in discrimination learning. In discrimination learning, students deal with familiar tonal patterns and rhythm patterns that may be presented in familiar or unfamiliar order. In inference learning, students deal with unfamiliar as well as familiar tonal patterns and rhythm patterns that are, through necessity, presented in unfamiliar order.

Discrimination learning and inference learning are not mutually exclusive, although discrimination learning serves as a readiness for inference learning. Moreover, there are five levels, some of which include sublevels, of discrimination learning, and there are three levels, all of which include sublevels, of inference learning. Each level and sublevel of learning serves as a readiness for and becomes part of the next higher level or sublevel of learning.

The first and most elementary level of discrimination learning is aural/oral. Using a neutral syllable, students hear, audiate, and sing familiar tonal patterns and they hear, audiate, and chant familiar rhythm patterns. The second level of discrimination learning is verbal association. Students hear, audiate, and sing familiar tonal patterns using tonal syllables (tonal solfege) and they hear, audiate, and chant familiar rhythm patterns using rhythm syllables (rhythm solfege) that they learned at the aural/oral level. Students also name the functions of the tonal patterns and rhythm patterns. The third level of discrimination learning is partial synthesis. Students recognize and name the tonality of a series of familiar tonal patterns, and they recognize and name the meter of a series of familiar rhythm patterns. The fourth level of discrimination learning is symbolic association. It has two subparts: reading and writing. Students audiate and read or write familiar tonal patterns and familiar rhythm patterns. The fifth level of discrimination learning is composite synthesis. It has two subparts: reading and writing. Students audiate and read or write series of familiar tonal patterns and familiar rhythm patterns.

The first and most elementary level of inference learning is generalization. It has three subparts: aural/oral, verbal, and symbolic. Aural/oral in discrimination learning and generalization-aural/oral in inference learning are parallel levels of learning: students engage in the

Outline of Skill Learning Sequence in Formal Instruction

DISCRIMINATION

AURAL/ORAL
VERBAL ASSOCIATION
PARTIAL SYNTHESIS
SYMBOLIC ASSOCIATION
Reading - Writing
COMPOSITE SYNTHESIS
Reading - Writing

INFERENCE

GENERALIZATION
Aural/Oral - Verbal - Symbolic
Reading - Writing
CREATIVITY/IMPROVISATION
Aural/Oral - Symbolic
Reading - Writing
THEORETICAL UNDERSTANDING
Aural/Oral - Verbal - Symbolic
Reading - Writing

same activities at both levels of learning except that in discrimination learning students deal only with familiar patterns, and in inference learning students deal with unfamiliar as well as familiar patterns. For the same reason, verbal association and partial synthesis in discrimination learning and generalization-verbal in inference learning are parallel levels of learning, and symbolic association and composite synthesis in discrimination learning and generalization-symbolic in inference learning are parallel levels of learning. The second level of inference learning is creativity/improvisation. It has two subparts: aural/oral and symbolic. At the creativity/improvisation-aural/oral level students hear, audiate, and create or improvise music that includes familiar and unfamiliar tonal patterns and rhythm patterns, using a neutral syllable, tonal syllables, or rhythm syllables. At the creativity/improvisation-symbolic level, students audiate, create or improvise, read symbols, and notate music that includes familiar and unfamiliar tonal patterns and rhythm patterns. The third level of inference learning is theoretical understanding. It has the same three subparts as generalization: aural/oral, verbal, and symbolic. The respective subparts of the generalization level and the theoretical understanding level are parallel. The differences in theoretical understanding as compared with generalization are 1) students discover why traditional names and definitions associated with music theory are used, and 2) only specific functions, such as letter names, time value names, intervals, and cadences that are typically associated with music theory are heard, audiated, performed, read, and written.

Given an understanding of music learning theory, the distinction between imitation and audiation can be made even clearer. Imitation is primarily associated with discrimination learning, whereas audiation is primarily associated with inference learning. Stated another way, if one hears something familiar and is capable of generalizing it to something unfamiliar, to that extent she is no longer imitating. She is clearly audiating.

Chapter Four

PREPARATORY AUDIATION AND MUSIC LEARNING THEORY

Music learning theory, in terms of preparatory audiation for young children who are still receiving structured and unstructured informal guidance in music, can be most readily understood if it is thought of in two parts. The first part, the actual music learning theory, constitutes a learning model. The second part, learning sequence activities, constitutes a teaching model. The learning model has a theoretical foundation. The teaching model has a practical foundation, and is based upon the learning model. The emphasis of this chapter is on the learning model. The emphasis of the remaining chapters will be on the teaching model.

Both the learning model and the teaching model deal with a process rather than a product. How a young child naturally uses his intuitive music aptitude, regardless of how rapidly or slowly he may progress from one type or stage of preparatory audiation to the other, is the core of the learning model. How a young child is given paced structured and unstructured informal guidance in music to develop his cognitive music achievement is the core of the teaching model. For a teacher or parent to use either the learning model or the teaching model effectively, he must understand both. The pace at which many children phase themselves through the sequence of the types and stages of preparatory audiation is usually not ideal. A child's inclination and his readiness to engage in a given type or stage of preparatory audiation do not always coincide.

There are two important differences between audiation, as it is typically associated with children who have emerged from music babble and are receiving formal instruction in music, and preparatory audiation, which is typically associated with children who have not emerged from music babble and are receiving structured and unstructured informal guidance in music. 1) Whereas the seven types and six stages of audiation described in Chapter Three are referred to as audiation, the three types and seven stages of audiation discussed in this chapter - acculturation, imitation, and assimilation - are referred to as preparatory audiation. The types and stages of preparatory audiation, which are the bases for both the learning model and the teaching model, serve as readinesses for the types and stages of audiation. The child's transition from preparatory audiation to audiation takes place at the junction of the seventh stage of preparatory audiation and the first stage of audiation. 2) The types and stages of audiation are distinctly different from the levels of music learning theory that are associated with older children, whereas the types and stages of preparatory audiation are themselves the levels of music learning theory that are associated with younger children. It must be understood, however, that a child's ability to engage in a given type or stage of preparatory audiation is more indicative of his musical age than of his chronological age. Musical age and chronological age are not necessarily related to each other. Moreover, a child is capable of engaging in either preparatory audiation or in audiation whether he is in the developmental music aptitude stage or in the stabilized music aptitude stage.

When a young child who is in music babble listens to music, he does not usually give systematic meaning to what he is hearing. He may dismiss what he is hearing, or he may deal with it simply in terms of acculturation. Further, he may be attending to, at most, only one of the various musical aspects that he may be hearing. All of those responses to music are associated with preparatory audiation, and together they represent the readinesses for him to learn to audiate so that he may audiate to learn. Depending upon his level of music aptitude, the extent to which a child phases through the various types and stages of preparatory audiation in structured and unstructured informal guidance will determine how well he will learn to engage in the types and stages of audiation in formal instruction.

The progression of the types of preparatory audiation from the first to the last and the progression of the stages within each type of preparatory audiation from the first to the last are sequential. It is for that reason that the types and stages of preparatory audiation on the one hand and the associated music learning theory on the other are one and the same. In contrast, the progression of the stages of audiation, not always from the first to the last, are sequential only within a specific type of audiation, and the types of audiation, each of which is related to a different level of its associated music learning theory, are not sequential. It is particularly important to remember that both the stages of preparatory audiation and the stages of audiation are hierarchical and cumulative. That is, each stage of preparatory audiation serves as a basis for and becomes part of the next higher stage of preparatory audiation, and each stage of audiation serves as a basis for and becomes part of the next stage of audiation.

A child may be capable of engaging in a higher type and a higher stage of tonal preparatory audiation while at the same time he may be capable of engaging only in a lower type and a lower stage of rhythm preparatory audiation. The reverse is also true. Just how long or short a time a child should engage in a given type and stage of preparatory audiation cannot be said with certainty. Not only musical differences but also emotional and physical differences among children contribute to such a lack of uniformity. A young child's levels of tonal and rhythm developmental music aptitudes and the interaction of those aptitudes with the degree of richness of his music environment play a dominant role in determining the rapidity with which a child will progress through the types and stages of preparatory audiation.

Regardless of a young child's level of developmental music aptitude or of his emotional or physical maturity, under no circumstances should he be rushed through the types and stages of preparatory audiation. During those important years, a child should not be forced to learn. He should be allowed and encouraged to explore and to absorb all that he is capable of exploring and absorbing. A child's preparatory audiation will develop most efficiently and appropriately if he is exposed early to music in as many tonalities and meters as possible. Under those circumstances, preparatory audiation will be enhanced by such a rich variety of sound. If anything, the child's reaction to variety in music represents good confusion. Good confusion is a result of the child's attending to the differences among songs and chants. Bad confusion is a result of the child's attending to the supposed continual sameness among songs and chants.

Children should progress through the types and stages of preparatory audiation sequentially, Although he may appear able, a child with high levels of developmental music aptitude should not be encouraged to progress more quickly through the sequence than one with low levels of developmental music aptitudes. A child with high levels of developmental music aptitudes should remain long enough in each type and stage of preparatory audiation to derive as much benefit from structured and unstructured informal guidance in music as his developmental music aptitudes will allow. Within a given period of time it is much more valuable for a young child to learn a great deal from

31

having engaged in one type or stage of preparatory audiation than to learn a little from having engaged in many types and stages of preparatory audiation. If a young child does not appropriately advance himself from one type of preparatory audiation to another or from one stage of preparatory audiation to another, the responsibility of deciding when to encourage him to move on must be undertaken by a knowledgeable adult.

It is not unusual for a young child to have the musical readiness but not the emotional readiness, or vice versa, to progress from one type or stage of preparatory audiation to another. Sometimes young children are reluctant to allow themselves to progress in preparatory audiation because of self protection; it is more comfortable for them to deal with something that is familiar than with something that is unfamiliar. The importance of having a knowledgeable adult to oversee the progress of a young child through the types and stages of preparatory audiation cannot be overemphasized. The adult must be aware that it will be a challenge to sustain the young child's attention in order for him to move forward from one type to another and from one stage to another of preparatory audiation. Of particular concern will be the young child who demonstrates an extreme in tonal developmental aptitude or rhythm developmental aptitude. Typically the child will choose to give more attention to his musical strength than to his musical weakness. The adult must be sure that the lower of the child's two developmental music aptitudes is given as much attention as the higher, if not more, in at least the child's initial exposure to structured and unstructured informal guidance in music.

Types of Preparatory Audiation

There are three types of preparatory audiation. They are acculturation, imitation, and assimilation. There are three stages of preparatory audiation within acculturation. There are two stages of preparatory audiation within imitation. There are two stages of preparatory audiation within assimilation. The types and stages of preparatory audiation are summarized in and are outlined at the end of this chapter. A detailed explanation of each type and stage of preparatory audiation is presented in order in the following three chapters.

32

Acculturation

A young child acquires music acculturation in much the same way that he acquires language acculturation: he does a great deal of listening and formulating. In language, for example, he begins to hear and to discriminate between the sudden shifts in "ba" and "da," and he begins to understand the different ways in which the two sounds are used. The more varied the speech that he listens to, the better he will learn to communicate when he is older. The young child's acquired listening vocabulary serves as a basis for the development of his babbling vocabulary, and for the later development of his speaking vocabulary. His speaking vocabulary serves as the basis for the development of his reading and writing vocabularies. So it is with music.

Ideally, the first stage of music acculturation takes place from birth to eighteen months. The sooner the young child engages in music acculturation, particularly before language development becomes so compelling that music acculturation may become of secondary importance to him, the better. It is late for a child to begin to engage in music acculturation when he is three years old, and it is almost too late for some children - those with exceptionally low developmental music aptitude - to begin to engage in music acculturation when they are five years old. The quality of acculturation, however, is as important as the age at which a child enters acculturation, and it is probably more important than the age at which a child leaves acculturation and is ready to engage in the next higher type of preparatory audiation.

In acculturation, the young child is exposed to the music of his culture through live and recorded sources in his environment. The young child bases his music babble sounds and movements upon the musical sounds that he hears and has heard in his environment. It is through acculturation that the young child develops the readiness to engage in imitation and assimilation. The more varied the music that he hears, that is, the richer his music environment and the more structured and unstructured informal guidance in music that he receives, the more he will profit from acculturation. Probably the young child benefits most in every type of preparatory audiation from an adult's singing and chanting to him and with him.

When a young child is engaging in acculturation, his attention is not continuous, nor is it always obvious. Nonetheless, he is what he hears and he becomes what he has heard. At times it may seem that a young child is not attending to music when he is receiving either structured or unstructured informal guidance in music. That, however, is usually not the case. The young child is aware of most of what he hears, whether or not he gives direct evidence of his awareness. The adult must expect, at best, only *a* response, not *the* response from a young child who is engaging in acculturation. Intention rather than attention should be fostered. It is an activity, not the act, that is important. It is through structured and unstructured informal guidance in music that a young child is led to develop the readiness to be able to audiate what he hears, and to be adequately prepared to deal later with imitation and assimilation in preparatory audiation.

During the first of the three stages of acculturation, the child responds to his environment by listening. During the second stage of acculturation, he makes music babble sounds and movements that are not particularly related to his environment. During the third stage of acculturation, he makes music babble sounds and movements in response to his environment. It is important that the teacher and parent be patient, and expect nothing immediate of the child who is phasing through music acculturation. Just as a child requires time to absorb his language environment before he can learn to speak, a child requires time to absorb his music environment before he can learn to sing, to chant, and to move musically.

Imitation

The transition from music acculturation to music imitation in preparatory audiation is a significant occurrence in the musical development of a young child. The younger a child is when he is prepared to make that transition, the better he will learn to imitate. If a child of any age engages in music imitation without the benefit of first having sufficiently engaged in music acculturation, his ability to engage in music imitation will be limited. On the other hand, as soon as a child engages in music imitation, his continued development in music acculturation (all three stages) typically begins to slow. That is unfortunate, because the development of a child's preparatory audiation and audiation ultimately depends upon the extent to which he develops his music acculturation. We never outgrow are need to engage in music acculturation. Even as adults, we are always engaging in some type of music acculturation.

In music acculturation, a child reacts almost without thought. In music imitation, a child acts with some purpose, musical or otherwise. Whether he imitates correctly or incorrectly, a child profits greatly from engaging in music imitation. Unless the child engages in music imitation, his ability to engage in music assimilation will be limited. It is the good confusion that the child experiences in the first stage of the imitation type of preparatory audiation that enables him to participate successfully in the second stage of the imitation type of preparatory audiation.

The first stage of the imitation type of preparatory audiation is best referred to as the first of the two transition stages within the seven stages of preparatory audiation. In that stage, the child is making his initial transition from preparatory audiation and music babble to audiation. He becomes aware, in terms of sameness and difference, that what he is singing and chanting is not what another child, a teacher, a parent or another adult is performing. In a sense, he is emerging from his egocentricity as a result of discovering that what he is singing and chanting in supposed imitation is actually not what another child or adult is singing or chanting. The realization that he is singing or chanting only what he is attending to, and not what another person is singing or chanting, is crucial for his further development in preparatory audiation. The child in his own way must become aware that he has been engaging in a sense of subjective preparatory audiation (what he communicates to himself) and that he must acquire a sense of objective preparatory audiation (what he communicates to others). Without that breakthrough, the child will not possess the proper understanding to proceed to the fifth stage of preparatory audiation, which is the second stage of the imitation type of preparatory audiation.

In the second stage of the imitation type of preparatory audiation, the child begins to imitate with some precision the tonal patterns and rhythm patterns that a peer or an adult is singing or chanting. As a result of "breaking the code" of the music culture that surrounds him, he is able to recognize and to discriminate among tonal patterns and to recognize and to discriminate among rhythm patterns as he attempts to imitate them. The quality as well as the quantity of the tonal patterns and rhythm patterns that the child is exposed to is of particular importance at this stage of preparatory audiation. As he is learning to imitate tonal patterns, he may be audiating the tonic of the keyality or the resting tone of the tonality in which the tonal patterns are being performed. Similarly, as he is learning to imitate rhythm patterns, he may be audiating the macro beats and/or micro beats of the meter in which the rhythm patterns are being performed. When a child engages concurrently in some combination of audiation and preparatory audiation, he usually is *audiating* syntax as a foundation for his *imitating* a tonal or rhythm pattern.

At the fifth stage of preparatory audiation, it is important that the child hear and perform different songs and different tonal patterns in a variety of keyalities and tonalities. The same song and tonal pattern, however, should always be heard and sung in the same keyality and the same tonality. Similarly, it is important that the child hear and perform different chants and different rhythm patterns in different tempos and meters, but the same chant and rhythm pattern should always be heard and chanted in the same tempo and the same meter. To ensure consistency of keyalities, tonalities, tempos, and meters, a cassette should be made of the familiar voice of an adult performing tonal patterns and rhythm patterns. Without such reinforcement of consistency, the young child will not recognize a pattern as being the same when it is performed in a different keyality, tonality, tempo, or meter.

Assimilation

The first stage of the assimilation type of preparatory audiation is referred to as the second of the two transition stages within preparatory audiation. During the first transition stage of preparatory audiation, which occurs in the imitation type of preparatory audiation, the child becomes aware that he is not coordinated with another person. During the second transition stage of preparatory audiation, which occurs in the assimilation type of preparatory audiation, the child becomes aware that he is not coordinated with himself. Specifically, in the sixth stage of preparatory audiation, the child becomes aware that his singing of tonal patterns is not coordinated with his body movement and breathing and that his chanting of rhythm patterns is not coordinated with his muscular movement and breathing. Without the realization that occurs in the first stage of the assimilation type of preparatory audiation, the child cannot adequately proceed to the seventh and final stage of preparatory audiation. And without passing through the seventh stage of preparatory audiation, the child will not be prepared to engage adequately in audiation activities as he emerges from music babble as a result of phasing through the stages of preparatory audiation.

36

In the seventh stage of preparatory audiation, the child learns to coordinate with some precision his singing of tonal patterns with his muscular movement and breathing, and his chanting of rhythm patterns with his muscular movement and breathing. The child learns to breathe appropriately in conjunction with movement when singing tonal patterns, and to appropriately direct the weight and flow of movement in conjunction with breathing when chanting rhythm patterns. He becomes aware of anacrusis, crusis, and metacrusis when he performs tonal patterns and rhythm patterns in familiar tonalities, keyalities, meters, and tempos. Given the breadth of experience which results from structured and unstructured informal guidance in music in the seven stages of preparatory audiation, the child naturally moves out of preparatory audiation and into audiation. He is able to learn to audiate as he listens to, performs, reads, writes, creates, and improvises music. Perhaps of greatest importance, the child is able to learn to perform more accurately, using his voice or an instrument, in ensemble as well as in solo. He is able to learn to accommodate and give objective musical meaning in his own audiation to what others are audiating and performing. The child will in time be capable of truly enjoying music, because he will be able to give meaning to music through audiation. His developmental music aptitude probably will have reached as high a level as hoped for by his teacher and parents. He is prepared to learn how to understand and to appreciate music as a musician, though not necessarily as a professional musician, throughout his life. When he is older, he will become part of the great audience that will demand that good music be performed under the best of conditions.

On the following page is a summary in outline form of the types and stages of preparatory audiation. It must be remembered that 1) the types and stages of preparatory audiation overlap, 2) the chronological ages are only approximations and that there are significant individual musical differences among children as a result of their music aptitudes, music experiences, and personalities, and 3) children may move from one type or stage of preparatory audiation to another without giving any outward evidence of when the change takes place.

Summary Outline of the Types and Stages of Preparatory Audiation

Type	Stage
ACCULTURATION Birth to age 2-4: engages with little consciousness of the environment.	**1 ABSORPTION:** hears and aurally collects the sounds of music in the environment. **2 RANDOM RESPONSE:** moves and babbles in response to, but without relation to, the sounds of music in the environment. **3 PURPOSEFUL RESPONSE:** tries to relate movement and babble to the sounds of music in the environment.
IMITATION Age 2-4 to age 3-5: engages with conscious thought focused primarily on the environment.	**4 SHEDDING EGOCENTRICITY:** recognizes that movement and babble do not match the sounds of music in the environment. **5 BREAKING THE CODE:** imitates with some precision the sounds of music in the environment, specifically tonal patterns and rhythm patterns.
ASSIMILATION Age 3-5 to age 4-6: engages with conscious thought focused primarily on self.	**6 INTROSPECTION:** recognizes the lack of coordination between singing and breathing and between chanting and muscular movement, including breathing. **7 COORDINATION:** coordinates singing and chanting with breathing and movement

Chapter Five

ACCULTURATION

It has been explained that music learning theory for children who have not emerged from music babble is different from music learning theory for children who have emerged from music babble. It also has been explained that the types and stages of preparatory audiation are the same as the levels of music learning theory for children who are still in music babble, whereas the types and stages of audiation are different from the levels of music learning theory for children who are no longer in music babble. Children who have not emerged from music babble engage in three types and seven stages of preparatory audiation. Children who have emerged from music babble engage in seven types and six stages of audiation.

Of the three types of preparatory audiation - acculturation, imitation, and assimilation - acculturation is fundamental. Children engage in acculturation before they engage in imitation, and they engage in imitation before they engage in assimilation. The three types of preparatory audiation are hierarchical and progressively cumulative, the extent of success with each higher type being dependent upon the extent of success with all types below it. So too are the stages of preparatory audiation sequential within each type. It is important that young children receive an abundance of the acculturation type of preparatory audiation. Without the necessary readiness that acculturation provides, their development in the imitation type, and later in the assimilation type, of preparatory audiation will be greatly restricted. Moreover, the acculturation type of preparatory audiation is requisite if young children are to acquire the appropriate readinesses for developing their singing voices and rhythmic movement. *The parent and teacher must continually keep in mind that immediate results in terms of music achievement should not be expected of children who are being guided in music acculturation. Moreover, children's progress in music acculturation cannot be rushed.* It may take eighteen months or longer before the benefit of guidance in music acculturation can be observed. The three stages within the acculturation type of preparatory audiation are discussed below in sequential order.

Shortly after birth, children become musically acculturated in varied ways. They may hear music played in the home or on the radio;

they may hear professional musicians in live performances on television or in more intimate circumstances; and most important, they may hear their parents, and perhaps sisters and brothers and other children, singing and chanting. As children engage in music acculturation, they learn to distinguish the sounds in their environment from the sounds that they themselves produce. They then learn to discriminate among sounds in their environment. As that process unfolds, they begin to change their role from being only hearers of sounds to being participators in the making of sounds.

Music acculturation, which takes place primarily in the home, and ideally during the first eighteen months of life, is a gradual process. As it occurs, a child moves from stage one to stage three of preparatory audiation. The more and the sooner a young child engages in the acculturation type of preparatory audiation, the sooner she will emerge from music babble. It is true that a kindergarten child who has not had much involvement with acculturation can emerge from music babble sooner than an eighteen month old child who is engaging in the acculturation type of preparatory audiation. However, although a child of kindergarten age can acquire music acculturation sooner than a much younger child, the very young child who acquires music acculturation will eventually profit more from formal music instruction when she is older than a child who acquires music acculturation after she is five years of age.

In stage one, children simply listen to music. In stage two, they randomly begin to sing, chant, and move in terms of music babble, but not in association with music that they are listening to or have listened to. In stage three, they sing, chant, and move in terms of music babble as they *attempt* to imitate what they are listening to or have listened to. In all three of those stages of the acculturation type of preparatory audiation, children learn primarily as a result of listening. In the imitation type of preparatory audiation, a child learns primarily as a result of the adult's first imitating her and then of her imitating the adult. In the assimilation type of preparatory audiation, the child learns primarily as a result of assimilating through coordination her chanting and body movement and assimilating through coordination her singing and body movement.

Recordings designed specifically for children are not recommended for developing music acculturation. Those which include a story-telling text are least beneficial. Typical adult records and live music in all music styles are recommended. Instrumental music, not vocal music, is most beneficial. The text in vocal music, like the text of a story recorded with music background, diverts the child's attention from the music itself. When listening to music with words, the child cannot directly focus on either the music or the words. The goal in music acculturation is to provide the child with unstructured informal guidance in music so that she may become familiar with the prevailing tonalities and meters of the music of her culture. Opportunities for assisting a child in becoming familiar with the language of her culture are abundant, and therefore need not be used in combination with music at the expense of the child's music acculturation.

The specific tonalities, keyalities, harmonies, meters, and tempos associated with the music that children hear are not important. What is important is that there is a diversity of tonalities, keyalities, harmonies, meters, and tempos among the pieces of music that they listen to. Children should listen to music in at least major, harmonic minor, mixolydian, and dorian tonalities, and in at least usual duple, usual triple, unusual paired, and unusual unpaired meters. Should children listen to an abundance of music in the same tonality and in the same meter, that type of overlearning will inhibit their learning with ease other tonalities and meters later when they engage in higher stages and types of preparatory audiation, and in audiation itself. With any type of music, however, it is more important that the children bond (become familiar and comfortable) with different tonalities and meters in music than that they bond with the adult who is associated with or is providing the music.

The tone quality of the music that children listen to should be pleasing and comforting. Certain instruments should not be given preference. A pleasant tone quality can be derived by a musician from any instrument. Because young children and adults tend to prefer the same tone qualities and to listen to the same types of music, parents should choose music for their children which they themselves find appealing.

41

Dynamics, timbre, tempo, and rhythm should be considered after a piece of music has been found to excel in tone quality. Whereas tone quality is a general and subjective term that refers to one's preference, timbre is a specific and objective term that refers to the unique sounds that can be produced on any one instrument or group of instruments. Recorded and live music should have frequently changing dynamics and timbre. *Abrupt*, not gradual, changes in tempo in the same piece of music are also desirable. The more the music has contrasting dynamic sections, contrasting timbre sections, and obviously contrasting tempo sections, the greater impression its sound will make on the children, and the more readily they will become familiar with the tonalities and the meters of their culture. Rhythm should be well articulated without over emphasis or exaggeration. Although a child should listen to different pieces of live and recorded music in different tempos, each piece of music should be performed at the same tempo every time it is heard. Tempo rubato and ritardandos in phrasing are acceptable. Long and exaggerated accelerandos and rallentandos, however, deprive young children of the needed stability that they derive from consistency of tempo.

The attention span of young children is very short. Only abrupt changes, especially in dynamics, timbre, and tempo, in the music being performed will encourage them to continually redirect their attention to the music. Music performed by large ensembles, such as orchestras and bands, is preferable to music performed by small ensembles or by a soloist. Popular music and folk music that contain excessive repetitive tonal patterns and rhythm patterns and that are always in the same tonality, the same meter, or both, are least preferable. Attempts to play what many authorities refer to as "classical" music for the child and to avoid all other music should not be given serious consideration. So-called good and bad music can be found in any musical style. Moreover, it may be written by the same composer.

It is important to remember that children should be given only unstructured informal guidance in listening to music. Under no circumstances should an effort be made to force a child to listen to what is being performed, nor should the playing of music be discontinued if the child does not appear to be attending to it. Of greatest value to young children is that they are consciously or unconsciously continuing to absorb the sounds of the music of their culture. There is little doubt that young children derive as much from listening to music when they appear not to be paying attention as when they appear to be paying attention to the music. In fact, the quality of the music listening experience can be just as great when children are moving around (active listening) as when they appear to be more attentive to the music (passive listening).

It is not possible to harm a child by allowing her to listen to too much music. Music, with low to moderate volume, may be made available to the child during all of her waking hours. It may serve as background music to whatever else is taking place. Moreover, when music is continuously played and is barely audible as a child sleeps, she will become more and more quickly musically acculturated than if she sleeps in silence.

With regard to live music, a child should be sung to and chanted to, and she should be made aware of the body movements of others as soon as possible. Parents, teachers, other adults, and children may sing, chant, and move for the child. Short songs and chants are best, *and they should be performed without words.* One, or at most two or three syllables with musical inflections, in full voice should be used throughout a song or a chant. The same syllables need not be used over and over again for the same song or chant, and, of course, different syllables may be used for different songs and chants. If the teacher or parent finds it necessary on occasion to use words, it should be for the following reasons: to give children directions for participating in desirable activities, such as movement activities, and, if necessary, to regain the interest of children as they are receiving unstructured and structured guidance in music. However, the use of words *while* performing the song or chant should be discontinued, before they become familiar, and replaced with syllables as soon as possible. Examples of songs and chants without words that may be used with children who are engaging in the acculturation type of preparatory audiation are presented on the following pages.

No attempt should be made to "teach" the child songs, as is typically done with older children in formal instruction. Children should not be expected to respond, either informally without precision or formally with precision, to the singing, chanting, or moving of an adult or other children. Nonetheless, they may respond or even attempt to perform a phrase or two of the song or chant. The objective, however, is not to have children begin to "learn" the song or chant; the objective is to expose children to the song or chant so that they can absorb its tonality or meter. Just as young children must do a great deal of listening to become

43

acculturated to their native language, so they must do a great deal of listening to music in order to become familiar with the music of their culture. To insist that children respond, or even to encourage them to respond to music according to cultural and adult standards before they enter the fourth stage of preparatory audiation, the first stage of the imitation type of preparatory audiation, will usually delay, or even prevent, their becoming musically acculturated. It would be better for a child in the first stage of preparatory audiation not to be sung to or chanted to at all than to be expected to respond to singing and chanting according to adult standards.

When exposing children to live vocal and instrumental music in the home, parents must take special care to be sure that if instruments are being played, they are well tuned. If an out of tune instrument is used consistently, children will begin to absorb that intonation as being characteristic of their culture. The more deeply such inappropriate intonation becomes ingrained, the less likely it will be that it can be corrected. If several out of tune instruments are heard from day to day, children will become hopelessly confused in, if not prevented from, trying to understand the music of their culture. In particular, if a piano is used by a child or an adult simply to explore sound, it must be well in tune. It should be periodically tuned by a professional piano tuner or not played at all. It would be best to remove a permanently out of tune piano from the home.

Stage Two of Preparatory Audiation

The second stage of the acculturation type of preparatory audiation takes place not long after the child has begun to engage in the first stage of preparatory audiation as described above. Some observers believe that the first and second stages of preparatory audiation occur almost simultaneously. The fact is that at least all adjacent stages of preparatory audiation overlap. Stage one of preparatory audiation ideally takes place from birth to eighteen months of age. Stage two of preparatory audiation ideally takes place between the ages of one and three. Nonetheless, even after a child begins to engage in activities associated with stage two of preparatory audiation, it remains very important that she be given continued unstructured informal guidance in listening to recorded and live music in the manner already described for stage one of preparatory audiation. Although there is some overlapping, stage two must be given emphasis as soon as the child has had ample

44

SONGS WITHOUT WORDS

CHANTS WITHOUT WORDS

exposure to music in stage one. The listening experiences of stage one, however, should be continued after the child begins to make babble sounds and movements as she enters stage two. In all stages of preparatory audiation, and particularly in the acculturation and imitation types, a child should never be forced to listen to or to participate in music. She simply should be encouraged and guided in exploring and absorbing the sounds of her environment.

Listening is the emphasis in stage one and participation is the emphasis in stage two of preparatory audiation. In stage two, the child begins to make babble sounds and movements. The babble sounds and the movements, which typically are not coordinated, are not necessarily an attempt by the child to imitate what she is listening to or seeing, or what she has listened to or seen. The child simply has the need to babble and to move, and she does so with her own meaning. To the extent that a child has her own (subjective) syntax, her babblings in sound and movement are characteristic of that syntax and usually not of the (objective) syntax of her culture. If there is meaning to what the child is doing, probably she alone, or another child who knows her very well, can understand what is being done.

Activities associated with stage two of preparatory audiation may take place in preschool as well as in the home. Regardless of what a parent does at home, the child's preschool experiences have a special value in stage two of preparatory audiation which cannot be duplicated in the home. It is through group interaction that the child learns a great deal about music as a result of listening to and observing other children of similar age as they attempt to sing, chant, and move.

The purpose of stage two of preparatory audiation is to continue to expose the child to music so that she will be better prepared to absorb the sound of the music of her culture in a more specific and complex manner than she did in stage one of preparatory audiation. The child makes babble sounds and engages in random movements in association with tonality and meter, the fundamental syntaxes of music. The parent and the teacher should encourage the child to make babble sounds and movements through unstructured informal guidance. The adult should not attempt to teach the child, and the child should not be expected to imitate, either subjectively or objectively, sounds and movements that the parent or the teacher makes. Only natural sounds and random movements that the child voluntarily engages in should be encouraged. The babble sounds and movements that the child makes are essential for her music development just as they are for her language development.

Although a child should continue to listen to recorded and live instrumental music in stage two of preparatory audiation, of greatest value to the child will be in having a parent and a teacher sing and chant to her and model movements for her. In stage two of preparatory audiation, the parent and the teacher should sing and chant *to*, not *with* the child. Singing and chanting *with* the child should be delayed at least until the child enters the imitation type of preparatory audiation. Short songs and chants without words in as many tonalities and meters as possible should be sung and chanted without instrumental accompaniment of any kind. When a guitar or a piano, for example, is played as the parent or teacher is singing, the child does not, and probably cannot, give her full attention to the adult's voice and the music. It is through learning only the melody performed, and only with the human voice, that the child begins to imitate and later to audiate the tonalities and the meters of her culture. The singing of specific tonal patterns and the chanting of specific rhythm patterns should not be introduced until stage three of preparatory audiation.

The parent or teacher should not force the child to move. That is, under no circumstances should the parent or teacher move the arms, legs, or any other part of the child's body for her. The parent or teacher, however, may move *with* the child, rhythmically tap the child, and hold the child in her arms as the parent or teacher herself is moving. For example, she may rock, either sitting or standing, when holding the child.

Songs and chants that are performed for the child should be short and repetitive, and should have neither words nor instrumental accompaniment. The parent or teacher should perform the songs and chants in a relaxed manner, with musical expression and phrasing. They should be performed throughout with one or two syllables. For example, the syllable "bum" may be used primarily for songs, and the syllable "bah" may be used primarily for chants. If too many syllables are used to sing the same or different songs and if too many syllables are used to chant the same or different chants, it can be expected that the child will pay more attention to the changes in syllables than to the musical aspects of the song or chant. To the child, too many different syllables, especially used in the same song, typically take on the character of a text.

Every effort should be made to sing the same song in the same keyality, for example, D, Eb, or G, every time it is sung to the child. To do otherwise confuses the child, because young children do not understand the concept of tonal transposition. There are three year old children who have had the benefit of a preschool music background who do not recognize a song without words as being the same one when it is sung in one keyality on one occasion and in another keyality on another. The higher the child's developmental tonal aptitude, the more confused she becomes when she hears a song sung haphazardly, that is, without concern for performing it in the same keyality. It is possible that unless a child hears the same song sung consistently in the same keyality until she has emerged from preparatory audiation and goes into audiation, her developmental tonal aptitude will be adversely affected.

A given song should always be sung in the same tonality as well as in the same keyality. If a song initially sung in major tonality is accidentally or purposely sung in minor tonality, for example, before a child has emerged from music babble, her preparatory audiation may become impaired. Of course different songs should be sung in different keyalities and in different tonalities.

Before singing a song to a child, the parent or teacher should perform softly on a well tuned guitar or keyboard instrument the beginning pitch, the resting tone, or a few pitches to establish for herself (not for the child) the keyality and the tonality of the song to be sung. Either of those instruments, or a tuning fork, a pitch pipe, or an electronic keyboard should be within easy access so that the teacher or parent may quickly sound a reference pitch or pitches. A toy instrument should not be used for that purpose. Rather than incorrectly guessing the keyality of a song, it would be better to wait and to sing the song with precision for the child at a later time.

The range within which a song is sung by the parent or teacher is important, particularly when a child is in the early stages of preparatory audiation. The lowest pitch of the song should not be below D, a major second above middle C, and rarely should it be higher than A, a major sixth above middle C. That is the initial audiation range within which a child begins to learn to audiate. The tessitura of a song, the range within which most of the pitches occur, is also important. If the range of a song exceeds the range described above, at least the tessitura of the song must be contained within the initial audiation range.

51

In addition to singing the same song in the same keyality and tonality every time that it is sung to the child, the parent or teacher should also sing the same song in the same meter and approximately, if not exactly, at the same tempo every time that it is sung to the child. Care must be taken not to change the meter or to alter the tempo of the song. The parent or teacher should, for self preparation, audiate or perhaps move to the tempo and the meter of the song before performing it. To sing the song at the same tempo every time that it is performed is not easy. For most persons it will be necessary to use a metronome, a wristwatch, a stop watch, or a clock to establish at least the approximate tempo at which the song should be performed.

It may be anticipated that a child will have a personal pitch and a personal tempo. They can be discovered by astute listening and observation on the part of the adult. Most children demonstrate different personal tempos for music, whether it is in usual meter or unusual meter. Also, the younger the child is, regardless of whether the music is in usual meter or unusual meter, she will typically associate her personal tempo with micro beats rather than with macro beats. At first, a child will pay greater attention to songs and chants that emphasize her personal pitch and her personal tempo. After a child has developed the security which comes with having her personal pitch and tempo reinforced, different pitches and tempos should be emphasized through the performance of a variety of songs and chants. A child's personal pitch and personal tempo are best taken into consideration on an individual basis by the parent in the home.

As with songs, when the meter and the tempo of a chant are performed incorrectly because they are given little or no thought by the adult before she performs the chant, the child's developmental rhythm aptitude, particularly if it is high, will be adversely affected. Her expectations will be unreasonably thwarted under such circumstances, and she will tend to ignore and not listen to what she is hearing rather than come to terms with what, in her estimation, is irresoluble confusion.

Young children prefer to listen to chants that are performed at a somewhat faster tempo than that which adults typically use. That could be a result of children audiating what the adult considers micro beats as their own macro beats. Nevertheless, as with songs, when chants are performed for the child, the meter and tempo of a given chant must be the same every time that chant is performed. The parent or teacher must give even greater attention to musical expression and phrasing when performing a chant than when performing a song. A lasting impression is made on a child's musical sensitivity through the performance of chants. Musical style is more easily conveyed to the child through chant than through song.

Because sensitive movement itself is perhaps the most neglected aspect of a child's music acculturation, the parent or teacher must model movement by using syllable sounds or by accompanying herself with song or chant. *The movement that is made should be relaxed, free flowing, and continuous.* Marching, clapping, or tapping is not recommended. The greatest attention can be expected from a child if the parent or teacher remains in place (does not walk or march around the room) while gently moving, and if she uses her torso, particularly her hips, rather than her limbs, when moving. If limbs are used, it is preferable to use arms and hands rather than legs and feet. As in stage one of preparatory audiation, unstructured informal guidance is the rule in stage two of preparatory audiation.

Stage Three of Preparatory Audiation

The typical child engages in stage three of preparatory audiation when she is from eighteen months to three years old. Although capable of more complex musical activities in stage three of preparatory audiation than in the first two stages of preparatory audiation, the child must nevertheless continue to listen to songs and chants without words. Listening to songs and chants without words is no less important, and perhaps more important, in stage three of preparatory audiation than in stages one and two of preparatory audiation. It is also important that children, especially those with high tonal and/or rhythm developmental aptitudes, be encouraged to begin, with encouragement by an adult but on their own initiative, to create their own songs and chants. Although those songs and chants may not make musical sense to the adult, they do make sense to the child, and they will prove to be of significant value to a child's music development.

At approximately eighteen months of age a child begins to speak in phrases and in sentences. She becomes confused when spoken words that are familiar to her (sometimes called speech rhythms) are included in a song or a chant and are performed with different rhythm, meter, and tempo from those that she is accustomed to hearing when the words are used in language communication. For that reason alone, mnemonics (the names of persons, places, or things) should never be used to teach rhythm patterns. The child becomes confused even when words are unfamiliar. Thus aspects of rhythm preparatory audiation, and even of audiation itself, if a child has not had the benefit of guidance in preparatory audiation, are compromised when songs and chants are performed with words. When a familiar song or chant that contains words is performed without words, she is inclined to think more about the missing words than about the music itself.

By the time a child is engaging in stage three of preparatory audiation, and preferably sooner, she should be listening to songs in at least major, harmonic minor, mixolydian, and dorian tonalities, and to at least songs and chants in usual duple, usual triple, unusual paired, and unusual unpaired meters. The more different tonalities and meters that the child listens to, the better she will eventually learn to audiate any one tonality and any one meter. Listening to less familiar tonalities, such as mixolydian and dorian, and to less familiar meters, such as unusual paired and unusual unpaired, actually increases a child's potential for relating to more familiar tonalities and meters and for developing her preparatory audiation and audiation skills. Contrary to common belief, if a child listens to songs only in major and harmonic minor tonalities and only in usual duple and usual triple meters, her preparatory audiation and audiation skills will be developed to a much lesser extent than if she listens to other tonalities and meters as well. The more opportunities a child has to make comparisons, the more and the better she will learn.

In stages one and two of preparatory audiation, the child receives unstructured informal guidance in music. When the child embarks upon stage three of preparatory audiation, she receives structured informal guidance in music. The structure is not centered around songs and chants. It is centered around tonal patterns and rhythm patterns. The intent is not to teach a child to imitate tonal patterns and rhythm patterns. That must wait until the imitation type of preparatory audiation is introduced. The intent is to encourage the child to participate in the singing of tonal patterns and the chanting of rhythm patterns. The patterns that the child sings and chants need not be the same patterns that the parent or teacher is singing and chanting. Moreover, the parent or teacher should not extract melodic patterns, which *combine* both tonal and rhythm aspects, from songs used in stages one and two of preparatory audiation and then perform them for the child. The child must not be expected or directed to imitate tonal patterns and rhythm patterns, or, of course, melodic patterns, with any degree of precision. It can be anticipated, however, that because of a child's experience with speech babble, speech itself, and movement, her rhythm development will sooner have more precision than her tonal development.

It is during the breath that precedes the performance of a tonal pattern that the audiation of that tonal pattern begins to take place. Without an adequate breath before a tonal pattern is performed, imitation, never audiation, will always be the natural consequence. Thus the adult must make the deep breath that she is taking before she sings the tonal pattern obvious to the child. As readiness for learning to audiate, the child should be encouraged to do the same.

A child's larynx is not set in place until she is about one year old. Although she is able to eat, drink, and breathe at the same time, the child cannot speak, sing, or chant as an adult does. She is capable of making noises only with glissandos (the blending of one pitch into another without breaks of silence - short pauses - between pitches). Such sounds are like those which dolphins and whales make. After a child's larynx is set in place she can be expected to make separations between sounds. In order for her to make use of that newly acquired ability, she must be familiar with the sounds, in music as well as language, that she is attempting to make. Thus it is important that a child hear as much music, particularly singing and chanting, as possible before her first birthday, and certainly before she is three years old. Also, when she hears the singing of tonal patterns and the chanting of rhythm patterns by the parent or teacher, the child should be encouraged to explore many sound possibilities with her voice. Such exposure and activities serve as readinesses for her learning to sing tonal patterns and to chant rhythm patterns with separated sounds at a later time.

It is recommended that the parent or teacher sing one or more songs for the child in major tonality immediately before singing tonal patterns in major tonality to the child, and that she sing one or more songs for the child in minor tonality immediately before singing tonal patterns in minor tonality to the child. In that way, the child will have the opportunity of audiating the syntax and of giving meaning to the tonal patterns in terms of the tonality in which they are being sung. Even though the child is not yet really engaging in imitation, the song and tonal pattern should always be sung in the same keyality and, of course, in the same tonality.

In stage three of preparatory audiation, when a child begins to sing tonal patterns, she will sing at the same time that the parent or teacher is singing. Soon she will begin to sing tonal patterns alone, usually *attempting* to copy or mimic, though she will not actually imitate what was sung by the parent or teacher. The child should not be expected to imitate tonal patterns with accuracy in stage three of preparatory audiation. She will attempt to do so in stage four of preparatory audiation, and she will do so successfully in stage five of preparatory audiation. When, however, the child in stage three of preparatory audiation spontaneously sings the resting tone of the tonal pattern that the adult is singing, that is a signal that the child must be moved immediately into stage four of preparatory audiation, the first stage of the imitation type of preparatory audiation. Most children learn to audiate a resting tone before they are able to imitate, let alone audiate, a tonal pattern.

Only tonal patterns in major tonality and minor tonality that move diatonically (by step) should be sung to the child in stage three of preparatory audiation. Each tonal pattern should include three pitches. The range of the tonal patterns should be in the child's initial singing and audiation range, from D above middle C to A a perfect fifth above. When two or more tonal patterns are sung in succession, there must be a pause (a silent separation) and a deep breath between the tonal patterns. Moreover, the pitches in each tonal pattern should be of the same length, and always sung legato (without silent separations between the pitches), not staccato (with silent separations between the pitches), until the child reaches at least stage four of preparatory audiation, at which time the pitches in a tonal pattern are sung staccato. At stage three of preparatory audiation, the child discovers the pitches in diatonic tonal patterns with her throat muscles as she is singing. At stage four of preparatory audiation, the child attempts to imitate the pitches in arpeggioed tonal patterns *before* she moves her throat muscles to sing those pitches.

The tonal patterns must not be sung with words. The same syllable, for example, "bum," is best used throughout a tonal pattern. Examples of tonal patterns in major tonality and minor tonality that are appropriate for use when a child is in stage three of preparatory audiation are presented on the following page. Though not notated in the examples, diatonic tonal patterns may also be multi-directional (move up and down)

56

as well as unidirectional (move up or down). Examples of multi-directional tonal patterns in major tonality are DO RE DO, DO TI DO, RE DO RE, and TI DO TI. Examples of multidirectional tonal patterns in minor tonality are LA TI LA, LA SI LA, TI LA TI, and SI LA SI.

Several considerations are involved in the choice of a neutral syllable for tonal patterns. It must be comfortable, easy to articulate, insure a relaxed jaw and tongue, and allow a maximum length of time for intoning correct pitch. There are a number of reasons to use "bum" for singing tonal patterns. The initial voiced consonant "b" requires a sung pitch for its articulation. That insures a healthy use of breath energy with the onset of the pitch, which then continues naturally into the vowel that follows. The slight movement of the jaw for "b", not unlike chewing, releases jaw tension which otherwise might interfere with good intonation. The neutral vowel requires no special tongue adjustment, and the "m" is a hum, which carries the sound into the next syllable without a break. A hum is the most gentle use of the vocal folds. If not forced (sung too loudly), it is easy to sing in tune, and it encourages a smooth (legato) transition between pitches. The inner surfaces of the lips are loosely and gently bounced together for both the "b" and the "m". It is important that the lips not be pressed together tightly, because that will tighten the muscles of the throat as well.

One or more rhythm patterns in usual duple meter and usual triple meter that include no more than *two underlying macro beats* should be chanted to the child who is in stage three of preparatory audiation. The rhythm pattern or patterns should include one or more macro beats or micro beats in addition to divisions and elongations of macro beats and micro beats. The rhythm pattern or patterns may include any number of durations, some of which may be different from one another. All durations in the rhythm pattern or patterns must be chanted on the same pitch with, of course, musical inflections. The rhythm pattern or patterns should be chanted both staccato and legato. They must not be chanted with words. It is best to use only one syllable, for example "bah," when chanting rhythm patterns. "Bah" is recommended not only because it begins with "b," but primarily because it allows the separation of pitches with the throat, thus insuring more control over articulation.

As with tonal patterns, the deep breath taken by the parent or teacher before the rhythm pattern or patterns are performed should be made obvious to the child. That is best accomplished if the duration occurring on

MAJOR TONALITY

MINOR TONALITY

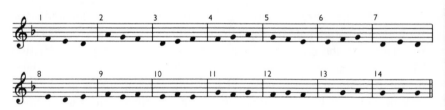

the second underlying macro beat is performed as a micro beat, and is followed by a micro beat rest. The child, too, must take a deep breath, without rushing or slowing the tempo, before she chants a rhythm pattern or patterns. To allow ample time for breathing without slowing the tempo, the tempo at which the rhythm patterns are chanted must be appropriate. When more than one rhythm pattern is performed within the two underlying macro beats, no pauses should be made or breaths taken between the patterns as they are being performed.

It is recommended that the parent or teacher perform one or more chants for the child in usual duple meter immediately before chanting rhythm patterns in usual duple meter to the child, and that she perform one or more chants for the child in usual triple meter immediately before chanting rhythm patterns in usual triple meter to the child. In that way, the child will have the opportunity of audiating the syntax and of giving meaning to the rhythm patterns in terms of the meter in which they are being chanted. Even though the child is not yet really engaging in imitation, the chant and rhythm pattern should always be chanted at the same tempo and, of course, in the same meter.

In stage three of preparatory audiation when a child begins to chant rhythm patterns, she will chant at the same time that the parent or teacher is chanting. Soon she will begin to chant rhythm patterns alone, usually *attempting* to copy or mimic, though she will not actually imitate what was chanted by the parent or teacher. The child should not be expected to imitate rhythm patterns with accuracy in stage three of preparatory audiation. She will attempt to do so in stage four of preparatory audiation, and she will do so successfully in stage five of preparatory audiation. When, however, the child in stage three of preparatory audiation spontaneously chants the underlying micro beats of the rhythm pattern that the adult is chanting, that is a signal that the child must be moved immediately into stage four of preparatory audiation, the first stage of the imitation type of audiation. Most children learn to audiate underlying micro beats before they are able to imitate, let alone audiate, a rhythm pattern.

Chants and rhythm patterns should be performed by the parent in the home at the child's personal tempo. If she moves slowly when chasing a ball, it is likely that she has a slow personal tempo. If she moves quickly when chasing a ball, it is likely that she has a fast personal tempo. Examples of rhythm patterns in usual duple meter and usual triple meter that are appropriate for use when a child is in stage three of preparatory audiation are presented on the following page. Each pattern is the length of one underlying macro beat. Because rhythm patterns make most sense to the child when they are performed within the length of two underlying macro beats, one of the notated rhythm patterns will need to be performed in conjunction with one macro beat or with two micro beats, or two of the notated rhythm patterns will need to be performed successively.

It is not desirable for the adult to perform tonal patterns immediately after rhythm patterns or to perform rhythm patterns immediately after tonal patterns for the child. It is best to separate the two types of patterns in structured informal guidance by performing one or more songs or chants between tonal patterns and rhythm patterns. So long as a song or a chant is performed in the proper tonality or meter beforehand, tonal patterns in major tonality may be sung shortly after tonal patterns in minor tonality, and vice versa, and rhythm patterns in duple meter may be chanted shortly after rhythm patterns in triple meter, and vice versa.

The most important reason why the typical child in stage three of preparatory audiation cannot be expected to be well coordinated or to be able to make precise movements is because of the restricted movement activities that have been forced upon her by adults and society. Thus the child must be given compensatory guidance in moving freely, continuously, and with flexibility. She should be encouraged to move for the same reasons that she is encouraged to chant. The child first should be given structured informal guidance in exploring for herself movement with different parts of her body. Then the parent or teacher should make movements with different parts of her own body, not the child's, and encourage the child to make a variety of movements by herself. The child should not be expected to imitate movements with any precision. The fact that she is attempting to imitate, which may be more appropriately described as her attempting to copy or mimic, is what is important. The child will find it much easier to move than to sing tonal patterns, and somewhat easier to move than to chant rhythm patterns. The more the child engages in free flowing movement, the sooner she will chant rhythm patterns. Movement activities and the chanting of rhythm patterns will also improve the child's ability to learn to sing tonal patterns. Movement helps the child bring subjective unconsciousness into objective consciousness.

The most effective type of compensatory movement for a child is for her to move her own arms and legs, as in swimming, and her entire body, as in rolling, continuously as she lies on the floor. Later, rocking from one foot to the other while standing is a simple movement with which all children can be expected to achieve almost immediate success. If a child can walk, she can rock. Natural movements that are confined to body parts from the waist up are most beneficial.Movements that incorporate and emphasize the use of body weight are best. Small muscle movements (as with fingers or even hands) should be avoided. Responding to the same and different movements in a variety of tempos will provide the child with the necessary readiness to attempt to chant simple rhythm patterns at stage three of preparatory audiation and to chant complex rhythm patterns at the higher stages of preparatory audiation.

The teacher or parent might improvise a story about a balloon, for example, in which the balloon is blown up, rises in the air, is blown around by the wind, begins to loose air, and finally falls gently to the ground. As the child pretends that she is the balloon, she will gradually engage in some free flowing and continuous movement. The most advantageous movement may occur when the child creates and acts out new parts to the story, perhaps using one or two scarfs.

A young child is unable to transpose in a musical sense. If a child listens to the same song in different keyalities or to the same tonal pattern in different keyalities, she will believe that she has heard two different songs or two different tonal patterns. If the child listens to the same chant in different tempos or to the same rhythm pattern in different tempos, she will believe that she has heard two different chants or two different rhythm patterns. Thus the adult should make cassette recordings of the songs, chants, tonal patterns, and rhythm patterns that have been performed for the child in stages one, two, and three of preparatory audiation. The recordings should be used in the home for the child to listen to when she chooses to do so. The use of the recordings will assure that the songs and tonal patterns will always be performed in the same keyality as well as in the same tonality, and that the chants and rhythm patterns will always be performed at the same tempo as well as in the same meter. Moreover, the child will respond more comfortably to and derive more benefit from a cassette recording if it is made with the voice that she has been listening to as she phases through stages one, two, and three of the acculturation type of preparatory audiation.

RHYTHM PATTERNS

USUAL DUPLE METER

USUAL TRIPLE METER

Chapter Six

IMITATION

There are two stages within the imitation type of preparatory audiation. The first stage is the fourth stage of preparatory audiation, and the second stage is the fifth stage of preparatory audiation. The fourth stage of preparatory audiation serves as a readiness for and is a transition to the fifth stage of preparatory audiation. The fourth stage, which takes place "outside" the child, because the child is comparing his performance with that of another person, is the first of two transition stages in which a child normally engages in preparatory audiation. The sixth stage of preparatory audiation, the first stage of the assimilation type of preparatory audiation, is the second transition stage of preparatory audiation. It takes place "inside" the child, because the child is comparing aspects of his own performance. In both transition stages, structured guidance, not teaching, is the rule.

It is not wise for a parent or teacher to encourage, let alone to force, a child to enter either of the two stages within the imitation type of preparatory audiation until the child has passed through the three stages of the acculturation type of preparatory audiation. Not only will the child find the imitation type of preparatory audiation difficult to deal with unless he has the necessary preparation that acculturation provides, but also he may develop anxiety and may find it impossible to learn how to imitate musically. Regardless of how old a child is when he begins to receive informal guidance in music, he must begin with the acculturation type of preparatory audiation. Under no circumstances should a child be taught to sing songs or be given lessons on an instrument unless he has had at least satisfactory experiences in the acculturation type of preparatory audiation and is at least phasing through the imitation type of preparatory audiation.

A child should have phased through the three stages of the acculturation type of preparatory audiation between birth and three years of age. The imitation type of preparatory audiation should end by the time a child is four years old. However, some children enter the first stage of the imitation type of audiation when they are as young as two years old, and some enter the second stage of the imitation type of preparatory audiation when they are as young as three years old. The level of a child's current developmental music aptitudes and the quality of his early music environment are the factors which determine when he will leave one preparatory audiation stage and enter another. It is not unusual for a child to be in an early stage of preparatory audiation tonally and in a later stage of preparatory audiation rhythmically. The reverse is also possible.

Stage Four of Preparatory Audiation

In stage four of preparatory audiation, which is the first stage of the imitation type of preparatory audiation, the child in a sense teaches himself. As a result of the appropriate guidance which the parent or teacher provides him, the child discovers that he is not imitating with musical accuracy what he has heard. Without such guidance, the chances are that he will not proceed to the second stage of the imitation type of preparatory audiation, within which he begins to imitate with musical accuracy. The parent or teacher must be patient with the child, and wait perhaps as little as only five minutes or as long as five weeks or months, to allow him to make his own discovery that what he is singing or chanting in supposed imitation is actually not what the parent or teacher or another child is singing or chanting, whether tonal patterns, rhythm patterns, songs, or chants. The same is true with regard to how a child is moving. The child must discover for himself, without being told, that how he is moving is not like how someone else is moving. The rule is to guide. Without the child's realization that his singing, chanting, and movements are not accurate, he may never understand the difference between accurate and inaccurate imitation. The sooner a child's personal pitch and tempo are reinforced by the parent at home or the teacher in school, the better prepared the child will be to enter the imitation type of preparatory audiation.

Specifically, in the first stage of the imitation type of preparatory audiation, the adult performs a pattern. It should be expected that the child will be able to audiate the resting tone of the tonality in which a tonal pattern is performed and the macro beats and micro beats in the meter in which a rhythm pattern is performed. The child, however, will not be able to imitate the pattern performed by the adult. Rather, he will automatically perform his own pattern. The parent or teacher listens to the pattern that the child sings or chants, he imitates the pattern that the child has sung or chanted, and then he encourages the child to sing or chant his own (not the parent's or teacher's) pattern once again as the parent or teacher sings or chants it with him. It is of the utmost importance at stage four of preparatory audiation that the parent or teacher imitate what the child sings and chants before the child is encouraged to attempt to imitate what the parent or teacher sings or chants. By the adult first imitating the child, the child becomes attentive to and acutely aware of what he is singing or chanting. What the child is singing or chanting becomes apparent ("real") to him as a result of hearing an adult perform what he has performed and is performing.

Some children move themselves from stage four to stage five of preparatory audiation. When the parent or teacher should make a conscious attempt to encourage a child who has not done so for himself to move out of stage four of preparatory audiation and into stage five of preparatory audiation cannot be stated with certainty. The adult must believe that the child has become aware that what he and the adult are performing are not the same. An "audiation stare" (explained further at the end of this section) is often given by the child as an indication that the transition should or will take place. Nevertheless, cautious judgment by the adult is needed in making that decision. The change from the fourth to the fifth stage of preparatory audiation may be made with rhythm patterns before tonal patterns or with tonal patterns before rhythm patterns. The time to make the change depends upon factors in addition to the child's awareness of sameness and difference, the most important of which is the level of the his tonal developmental aptitude if the change is to be initiated with tonal patterns and singing, or the level of his rhythm developmental aptitude if the change is to be initiated with rhythm patterns and chanting. A child's maturity and self confidence are also relevant. It is important to remember that once a child begins to attempt to imitate what the parent or the teacher has performed, he will also want to create tonal patterns and rhythm patterns spontaneously, particularly when other children are present and when he thinks that no adult is present or listening to him. It will usually take him some time to begin to attempt to imitate patterns in the presence of the parent or the teacher.

As in the third stage of preparatory audiation, in the fourth and fifth stages of preparatory audiation there are specific tonal patterns and rhythm patterns that are to be sung and chanted to the child. The specific patterns that are taught in the fourth and fifth stages of preparatory audiation are different from those that are taught in the third stage of preparatory audiation. First the tonal patterns and then the rhythm patterns will be described. As in the acculturation type of preparatory audiation, the tonal patterns are sung with the syllable "bum" and the rhythm patterns are chanted with the syllable "bah."

Diatonic patterns are primarily associated with discrimination, whereas arpeggioed patterns are primarily associated with recognition, imitation, and audiation. The tonal patterns that are used in the imitation type of preparatory audiation are of the arpeggioed type; they are not diatonic. All of the pitches in an arpeggioed tonal pattern except "SO to FA" and "FA to SO" in major tonality and "MI to RE" and "RE to MI" in minor tonality move by skip and not by step. Specifically, arpeggioed tonal patterns should include at least two, not more than four, and typically three, pitches. It is important that the child first be exposed to and respond to tonic function tonal patterns which include only two pitches. The tonic function tonal patterns which include two pitches, ascending and descending perfect fourths and fifths, include only "DO and SO" in major tonality and only "LA and MI" in harmonic minor tonality. The child will typically respond first to the ascending perfect fourth; next, to the descending perfect fourth; next, to the descending perfect fifth; and finally, to the ascending perfect fifth. Although the tonal patterns are arpeggioed, the child nevertheless becomes aware of the "half step" relationship of the leading tone to the resting tone as a result of his continually audiating the resting tone as he is imitating a tonal pattern.

In major tonality, any arrangement of "DO MI SO," two or three pitches, is used as a tonal pattern to represent tonic function, and any arrangement of "SO TI RE FA," two, three, or four pitches, is used as a tonal pattern to represent dominant function. In harmonic minor tonality, any arrangement of "LA DO MI," two or three pitches, is used as a tonal pattern to represent tonic function, and any arrangement of "MI SI TI RE," two, three, or four pitches, is used as a tonal pattern to represent dominant function. The child should not be exposed to and should not be expected to respond to 1) tonic function tonal patterns that include three pitches before he has been exposed to and has responded to tonic function tonal patterns that include two pitches, 2) dominant function tonal patterns before he has been exposed to and responded to tonic function tonal patterns, 3) dominant function tonal patterns that include three pitches before he has been exposed to and has responded to dominant function tonal patterns that include two pitches, and 4) tonal patterns which includes four pitches before he has been exposed to and has responded to tonal patterns that include three pitches. Tonal patterns

TONAL PATTERNS

MAJOR TONALITY

MINOR TONALITY

67

should be sung with the consistent use of a syllable, such as "bum." Examples of tonal patterns in major tonality and minor tonality that are appropriate for use when a child is in stages four and five of preparatory audiation are presented on the following pages.

During every presentation, songs in at least major tonality and minor tonality must be sung to the child before tonal patterns are sung to him. One or more songs in major tonality should be sung immediately before tonal patterns in major tonality are sung, and one or more songs in minor tonality should be sung immediately before tonal patterns in minor tonality are sung. It is not necessary to establish tonality for the child, though it usually is for the adult, before a song is performed. Pentatonic songs should not be used, because they do not include a leading tone (the seventh step of the scale). The child should not be expected to learn the songs. He should at most learn only to recognize them. Words must not be used with the songs, and the tempo of the songs should be neither too slow nor too fast. The same songs that were used for the acculturation type of preparatory audiation may be used for the imitation type of preparatory audiation.

It is not necessary to perform songs that include the tonal patterns that are to be sung after the songs are performed, or to sing tonal patterns that are found in the songs that the child hears performed before the tonal patterns are to be sung. Tonal patterns used for the imitation type of preparatory audiation are sung staccato (separated, not short) and not legato as was done for the acculturation type of preparatory audiation.

There is a difference between the speaking voice and the singing voice of every child, regardless of chronological age. Although the range of the voice is an aspect of that difference, the more important difference is the quality of the voice. Because the vocal folds are thicker for speaking than for singing, the speaking voice sounds somewhat heavier than the singing voice. In speech, the vocal folds are stretched very little, and the larger mass vibrates more slowly. If the pitch rises beyond customary speaking range without a quality change, the voice will sound forced and strained. In singing quality, however, the sound is lighter, because the vocal folds are thinner and more flexible, and they vibrate more quickly for higher pitches. Lower pitches are softer when sung in singing voice quality.

68

One of the most efficient ways to help a young child discover his singing voice is by showing him how to yell the word "hung" and then, while still yelling, quickly change the "hung" to "bum." The pitch or pitches that the child sings are irrelevant for the child to discover his singing voice. The singing of appropriate pitches is taken care of as the child is learning to imitate tonal patterns.

The range of the speaking voice and the range of the child's pseudo singing voice overlap. In time, the experienced child's singing voice covers the range of approximately A below middle C to G above middle C. The inexperienced child's singing voice, the initial singing voice, extends from only D above middle C to A above middle C. Thus some children may thought to be singing when in fact they are speaking at the top of their speaking range. Whether a child is actually singing or speaking is determined by the quality of his voice rather than by how "high" his voice may be pitched. If a child continually attempts to sing in his speaking voice, he will not develop the necessary audiation skill to profit from the higher stages of preparatory audiation.

Tonal patterns for the imitation type of preparatory audiation should be sung for the child in the initial singing range, which is identical to the initial audiation range. (That range, as explained, is from D above middle C to A a perfect fifth above.) Some dominant function patterns in both major and minor tonalities in the recommended keyality of D will need to exceed that range, but they should not do so by more than a half step or a whole step. It is important that the keyalities, and of course the tonalities, in which each pattern is sung to the child remain consistent from day to day as well as during the same day. As with stage three of preparatory audiation, care must be taken to be sure that a pause is made between tonal patterns that are sung to the child, and that a deep breath is taken by the adult as well as the child before a tonal pattern is sung.

The length of the specific rhythm patterns to be used in stage four of preparatory audiation should be *four underlying macro beats* rather than only two underlying macro beats as used in stage three of preparatory audiation. In every rhythm pattern, the first, second, and fourth underlying macro beats should correspond to one macro beat or two micro beats in terms of melodic rhythm, whereas the third underlying macro beat should correspond to something other than one macro beat or two micro beats in terms of melodic rhythm. Children are most comfortable with a rhythm pattern that has only a macro beat superimposed on the fourth underlying macro beat. The melodic rhythm of the third underlying macro beat should include one or more divisions and/or elongations of micro beats. Rhythm patterns that may be superimposed on the third underlying macro beat are the same as those that were described for use in the acculturation type, the third stage, of preparatory audiation. Rests should not be used, and divisions, rather than elongations, should be emphasized on the third underlying macro beat. Examples of rhythm patterns in usual duple meter and usual triple meter that are appropriate for use when a child is in stages four and five of preparatory audiation are presented on the following page. It will be noticed in the examples that the third macro beat is always notated as a rest, indicating that a melodic rhythm pattern must be superimposed on that underlying macro beat.

The tempo of rhythm patterns should not be too slow or too fast. When guiding only one child, it would be best for the parent or teacher to adapt the tempo at which the rhythm patterns are chanted to the child's personal tempo. The tempo at which the same rhythm patterns are chanted should remain consistent from day to day. All rhythm patterns should be chanted in a variety of styles.

During every presentation, chants in at least usual duple meter and usual triple meter are sung or chanted to the child before rhythm patterns are chanted to the child. One or more chants in usual duple meter should be performed immediately before rhythm patterns in usual duple meter are performed, and one or more chants in usual triple meter should be performed immediately before rhythm patterns in usual triple meter are performed. It is not necessary to establish meter for the child, though it usually is for the adult, before a chant is performed. The child should not be expected to learn the chants. He should learn only to recognize them. Words must not be used with the chants. The tempo of the chants should be neither too slow or too fast.

It is not necessary to make an effort to perform songs and chants that include the rhythm patterns that are to be chanted after the songs and chants are performed, or to chant rhythm patterns that are found in the songs and chants that the child hears performed before the rhythm patterns are to be chanted. Pauses should not be made between the rhythm patterns. It is necessary, however, to be sure that a deep breath is taken by the adult as well as by the child before every rhythm pattern is chanted. Rhythm sticks, drums, xylophones, for example, should not be

RHYTHM PATTERNS

USUAL DUPLE METER

USUAL TRIPLE METER

used either to teach or to accompany the chants that are being performed. The same chants that were used in the acculturation type of preparatory audiation may be used in the imitation type of preparatory audiation.

It is important that the child observe an adult moving in an artistic manner and that the child attempt to move in the same way at stage four of preparatory audiation. No attempt should be made to move the child's limbs for him. The adult may move with the child as they hold hands and also when the child and adult are moving independently. Neither the adult nor the child should clap hands. The best types of movement are made 1) when the knees are bent and straightened continuously while standing and 2) when the hips are moved continuously from side to side while kneeling with arms and hands placed on the thighs or moving freely in space. The use of recorded music for movement activities is not recommended. The adult should simply chant with a single syllable while moving. The child, however, should not be encouraged to chant as he is moving.

There are signs that the child gives when he is ready to leave the fourth stage of preparatory audiation and move into the fifth stage of preparatory audiation. Primary among them is the "audiation stare." The child will stare for a few seconds at the parent, teacher, or another person as the awareness comes that there is a difference between his singing or chanting or moving and someone else's. That is the first glimpse of discrimination; the realization of same or different. The child may also open his mouth and tilt his head. In a sense, the child is attempting to enter the world of audiation. At this point, the child does not know how to correct his singing, chanting, or moving; thus he cannot begin to enter the world of audiation. He knows only that something is not quite right. That may be the most important moment in the child's music education. It is up to the parent or teacher to seize the moment and to offer the child the most appropriate unstructured informal guidance to help him solve the problem for himself.

The time it takes for a child to move from the moment of the audiation stare to the threshold of the second stage of the imitation type of audiation is usually much longer than from the time the child enters the first stage of the imitation type of preparatory audiation to the time that he gives evidence of the audiation stare. How the parent or teacher may take best advantage of the child's discovery that there is more than a self, and to assist the child in strengthening and sustaining that discovery,

72

that is, how to appropriately shepherd him from the point of self realization to the beginning of the second stage of the imitation type of audiation, is described below.

Stage Five of Preparatory Audiation

In stage five of preparatory audiation the child first attempts to enter and to participate successfully in the adult's world of music in terms of the tonalities and meters of the culture that surrounds him. The child is able to meet the challenges that face him in stage five of preparatory audiation because of the readiness provided him by the first four stages of preparatory audiation. The importance of the first three stages of preparatory audiation in particular cannot be overestimated. It is not possible for a child to recapture what has been lost in his potential to learn to audiate if he is taken directly to stage five of preparatory audiation and expected to imitate with precision what another is performing. Though it must not be carried to an extreme, a child should be so guided as to remain in each of the first three stages of preparatory audiation as long as possible. That is perhaps even more important for a child with high overall developmental music aptitude than for one with low overall developmental music aptitude. Contrary to the opinion of many, a child with high overall developmental music aptitude needs a great deal of guidance and instruction. In order for such a child to use fully his music aptitude to make culturally acceptable inferences (to teach himself), guidance and instruction in the first three stages of preparatory audiation must be abundant as well as varied.

As explained, in stage four of preparatory audiation, a child usually sooner or later indicates through facial expression or movement that he is aware that the tonal pattern that he is singing (in a singing voice quality) or that the rhythm pattern that he is chanting is not the same as the pattern that the adult is singing or chanting. That is, he discovers that he is not imitating the pattern that is being or has been performed by the adult. At that point, the child should be phased into stage five of preparatory audiation in the following manner. The adult sings a tonal pattern. The child attempts to imitate it. Then the adult immediately imitates the tonal pattern that the child performed, sings the resting tone of the tonality that was originally established, and then repeats the original tonal pattern. If the child is using his speaking voice rather than his singing voice as he attempts to sing the tonal pattern, he should be given guidance in finding his singing voice. In the case of a rhythm pattern, the adult chants a rhythm pattern. The child attempts to imitate it. Then the adult immediately imitates the rhythm pattern that the child performed, chants two sets of micro beats in the meter that was originally established, and then repeats the original rhythm pattern.

There should be no concern about whether the pattern is "right or wrong." The adult must imitate the child's pattern as closely as possible. That is, the adult should imitate the pattern that the child has performed, regardless of its keyality, tonality, melodic contour, tempo, meter, or melodic rhythm, or of the simplicity or complexity of its construction. The adult should continue the process of imitating the child's pattern, reestablishing syntax, and repeating the original pattern as long as the child's attention is sustained. Continuous eye to eye contact between the child and the adult during the entire process is of great importance. As a result, the child's attention is held, and thus he is more likely to concentrate on listening.

The parent or teacher must use judgment along with cautious observation and evaluation as he is working with the child in stage five of preparatory audiation. The adult must be sensitive to children who demonstrate atypical music behavior and must compensate for or wisely use that behavior in the instructional process. A child may be attempting to imitate the adult's tonal pattern in his own subjective keyality and/or tonality or the adult's rhythm pattern in his own subjective tempo and/or meter. Or, at the other extreme, a child with exceptionally high developmental music aptitude may be audiating the objective keyality and/or tonality or the objective tempo and/or meter of the adult's pattern in terms of the adult's music syntax, but may nevertheless be unable to imitate the adult's pattern. It is also possible that although a child is audiating a resting tone, he is able only to sing the dominant pitch associated with the given tonality, and although he is audiating macro beats, he is able only to chant micro beats associated with the given macro beats, or vice versa. Children in stage five of preparatory audiation find tonal patterns in major tonality as easy to comprehend as tonal patterns in minor tonality. Children initially find rhythm patterns in usual duple meter easier to comprehend than rhythm patterns in usual triple meter. The longer the span of time between recurring macro beats (the slower the tempo), the more control the child must sustain in imitation when he is performing rhythm patterns.

74

It may be helpful to know, when working with a child who is entering stage five of preparatory audiation, that although the typical child initially performs a pattern different from the one that the adult is performing or has performed, it is actually easier for the child to audiate two tonal patterns or two rhythm patterns that sound the same than to audiate two tonal patterns or two rhythm patterns that sound different. After a child is able to imitate patterns, the adult should emphasize difference rather than sameness in patterns by exchanging patterns with the child. The child will find it difficult to purposefully perform different patterns, however, if he is not first able to perform through imitation a pattern that an adult performs. Moreover, the child finds it easy to audiate the difference between two pitches in a tonal pattern when they constitute a large interval, and difficult to audiate the difference between two pitches in a tonal pattern when they constitute a small interval. With the exceptions of "DO and SO" in major tonality and "LA and MI" in minor tonality, the child finds it easy to sing two consecutive pitches in a tonal pattern that constitute a small interval but difficult to sing two consecutive pitches in a tonal pattern that constitute a large interval.

The confusion that the child experiences as he engages in stage five of preparatory audiation is good confusion. When the child is unable to imitate the adult's pattern correctly, that is no cause for alarm. That the child is attempting to perform the pattern is an indication that he is learning. Initially, a correct response is more likely than not to follow an incorrect response.

As with previous stages of preparatory audiation, the adult must take a deep breath before he performs a pattern. The child must be encouraged to do the same. That is the case for both tonal patterns and rhythm patterns. The breath provides for the pattern to be generalized and summarized in preparatory audiation. That process becomes less pronounced and more natural when the child emerges from preparatory audiation into audiation itself.

Tonal patterns of only two pitches which include the tonic function "DO and SO," either as a fourth or a fifth, in major tonality, and which include the tonic function "LA and MI," either as a fourth or fifth, in minor tonality, must be introduced to and successfully performed by the child before tonic and dominant function tonal patterns which include three or four pitches are introduced and taught at stage five of preparatory audiation. Tonic patterns should be introduced before dominant patterns, and dominant patterns with only two pitches should be introduced before dominant patterns with three and four pitches. The syllable "bum" should be used when performing tonal patterns.

Rhythm patterns *which include at least one or more divisions of a micro beat superimposed on the third underlying macro beat of a pattern* are chanted for the child in stage five of preparatory audiation. A pattern which includes one or more divisions of a micro beat superimposed on the third underlying macro beat and only a macro beat superimposed on the fourth underlying macro beat quickly develops imitation in stage five of preparatory audiation. The syllable "bah" should be used when performing rhythm patterns. Mnemonics should not be used to perform rhythm patterns.

Patterns on the one hand and songs and chants on the other are designed to serve different purposes in the development of preparatory audiation. It is important that the child not be encouraged or expected to imitate a part of or an entire song or chant that is used to establish the keyality and tonality of the adult's tonal patterns or the tempo and meter of the adult's rhythm patterns. The child should be encouraged and expected to imitate only tonal patterns and rhythm patterns.

The child learns to discriminate among different tonalities and tonal patterns and among different meters and rhythm patterns in stages one, two, and three of preparatory audiation. The child learns to recognize different tonalities and tonal patterns and to recognize different meters and rhythm patterns in stages four and six of preparatory audiation. The child learns to imitate tonal patterns and to imitate rhythm patterns in stages five and seven of preparatory audiation. Imitation serves as the readiness for the child to learn to audiate after he leaves stage seven, the final stage of preparatory audiation. Unless the child has an idea of what he should be audiating as a result of his being able to discriminate, recognize, and imitate, and before he attempts to perform what he is supposedly audiating, he will not learn to audiate effectively.

No attempt is made to teach to the individual musical differences among children before stage five of preparatory audiation. The individual musical differences among children and the musical strengths and weaknesses (tonal versus rhythm) of a child when taught in a group or individually must begin to be taken into consideration at the fifth stage of preparatory audiation. That is, both normative and idiographic assessment are important.

In group guidance and instruction, it is not a matter of which patterns are easier or more difficult to learn in terms of guidance relative to normative assessment. The same patterns are taught to all children without regard to their levels of tonal developmental aptitude and rhythm developmental aptitude in stage five of preparatory audiation. It is the adult's responsibility to allow the child with a lower music aptitude to hear patterns repeated as many times as necessary in order for him to learn them well enough to imitate them. The child with higher developmental music aptitude will acquire a larger vocabulary of patterns than will the child with lower developmental music aptitude. That is to say that the child with higher developmental music aptitude will learn more patterns than will the child with lower developmental music aptitude as a result of the child with higher developmental music aptitude learning more quickly. Specifically, it may be expected that a child with higher tonal developmental aptitude will learn to imitate more tonal patterns than will a child with lower tonal developmental aptitude, and that a child with higher rhythm developmental aptitude will learn to imitate more rhythm patterns than will a child with lower rhythm developmental aptitude.

When adapting group instruction to the individual musical differences among children, it is not unusual for some children to be responding to patterns at a lower level of learning while at the same time some children are responding to patterns at a higher level of learning. For example, some children may still be engaging in stage three of preparatory audiation through the use of diatonic patterns while other children are engaging in stage four or stage five of preparatory audiation through the use of arpeggioed patterns. In adapting music instruction to the individual musical differences among children in preparatory audiation, it is a matter of the number of patterns and the type of patterns to which a child is exposed in addition to the type of response expected of a child. In audiation, adapting music instruction to the individual musical differences among children is a matter of only the number of patterns and the difficulty level of the patterns to which a child is exposed.

With regard to individual guidance and teaching in terms of idiographic assessment, the lower of the child's two developmental music aptitudes, tonal or rhythm, should be given initial attention. If the child has a lower tonal developmental aptitude than a rhythm developmental aptitude, emphasis must be placed on the teaching of tonal patterns. That is not to say that rhythm patterns should not be taught. It is simply a matter of which type of patterns, tonal or rhythm, will receive initial attention and emphasis. As soon as the child's lower of the two developmental music aptitudes begins to rise, the other developmental music aptitude must be attended to through the teaching of corresponding patterns so that its level will at least be maintained, and perhaps increased.

When adapting instruction to children's individual musical differences, the intent is not to deny any child the opportunity to engage in any type or stage of preparatory audiation. It is rather a question of how much and when. Perhaps the following analogy of the number of patterns one is exposed to with the quantity of liquid one has access to may help in making that concept clear. Consider two containers, one which holds a quart of liquid and the other a gallon. If both containers are filled with cream rather than the larger one with cream and the smaller one with skim milk, both, of course, will be holding liquid of equal quality. The only difference will be that one who has access to the gallon container will have the benefit of more liquid than one who has access to the quart container.

Audie, a developmental music aptitude test described in Chapter Two, should be administered to children three and four years old if they are engaging in at least stage four, and preferably stage five, of preparatory audiation. If the children are older, either the *Primary Measures of Music Audiation* or the *Intermediate Measures of Music Audiation*, both being developmental music aptitude tests, may be used. The results of a valid music aptitude test serve well as an objective aid to an adult's subjective opinion about a child's music potential and the progress that the child should be making.

When a child's ability to imitate patterns has been developed, the adult begins to engage the child in creating patterns. The sooner the child is able to create his own patterns in response to the adult's patterns, *and is aware that he is purposely not imitating the adult's pattern*, the better prepared he will be to engage in the acculturation type of preparatory audiation and audiation itself at a later time. The adult should not be concerned if the child's creative tonal pattern response is in a different keyality or tonality, or both, or if the child's creative rhythm pattern response is in a different tempo or meter, or both, from his own. The more a child becomes aware of the differences between his pattern and that of the adult's, the more beneficial the activity will prove to be.

In addition to chanting rhythm patterns at stage five of preparatory audiation, the child should engage in movement activities similar to those he engaged in at earlier stages of preparatory audiation. What is most advantageous to the child is for him to move his body with continuous motion. He should remain in place and continually move at least one part, preferably an upper part, of his body. The teacher or parent may initially assist the child in feeling continuous movement by rocking him, but not by moving parts of his body for him. Very young babies move gracefully with continuous movement, but they soon lose that ability. It is most beneficial for the child when the teacher or parent finds a way to help him recapture the feelings that he had when he moved as an infant.

The child should not be directed to clap or march or to attempt any other type of movement that encourages such discrete actions. He needs to learn to conceptualize rhythm as time punctuated by beat groupings rather than as beats establishing time. Clapping, marching, walking, running, skipping, and galloping should not be undertaken by the child in learning sequence activities at least until he enters stage six of preparatory audiation.

The adult can create games which will assist and guide the child in achieving sustained movement. The adult may ask the child to demonstrate what a tree does when the wind is blowing and to draw circles in space with different parts of his body. Words may be used to give direction to movements, particularly those taken from the child's life experiences, as well as to describe the game. It is important for the adult to continuously and softly chant in legato style the syllable "bah" on macro beats in a moderate to fast tempo as the child sustains continuous movement. The child should not be told to chant as he is moving. On the other hand, if the child chooses to chant as he is moving, he should not be stopped from doing so.

Effort motions, which are time, space, weight, and flow, in terms of movement, should be modeled for the child. Time may be fast or slow; space may cover a small, medium, or large area; weight may be light or heavy; and flow may be direct or indirect. As the adult is modeling for the child, he should be combining at least two of the effort motions. Time and space are basic, whereas weight and flow are more sophisticated. It is not possible to engage in motion that reflects weight and flow without also engaging in motion that reflects time and space. In order for a child to move with sustained motion and to remain relaxed, weight, flow, or both, must be combined with time and space. The adult need not concern himself with monitoring the child's breathing as he is engaging in movement. Appropriate breathing is a natural outcome of relaxed movement. It will be helpful for the adult to remember while guiding and instructing the child in movement activities that the type of movement the child engages in is a reflection of his inner being.

Chapter Seven

ASSIMILATION

There are two stages within the assimilation type of preparatory audiation. The first is the sixth and the second is the seventh and final stage. The sixth stage serves as a readiness for and is a transition to the seventh. The first transition stage, which is the first stage within the imitation type of preparatory audiation, and the second stage, which is the first stage within the assimilation type of preparatory audiation, are equally important. Without the readiness of the first transition stage, however, a child will not appropriately approach and pass through the second transition stage to the final stage of preparatory audiation. Structured informal guidance, in contrast to unstructured informal guidance, is emphasized in both transition stages of preparatory audiation.

Unless a child learns to compare what she is performing with how she is moving in the sixth stage of preparatory audiation and then learns to assimilate what she is performing with how she is moving in the seventh stage of preparatory audiation, it will not be possible for her to engage in audiation itself. It is impossible to say how long a child may be expected to remain in stage six of preparatory audiation. Individual differences are great. A child with high music aptitude may pass through the second transition stage of audiation within a matter of minutes, whereas it may take a child with low music aptitude weeks or months. Moreover, a child may advance to stage seven of preparatory audiation rhythmically while still remaining in stage six of preparatory audiation tonally. Of course the reverse is also possible.

The preparatory audiation *stage* that a child is currently engaging in is much more relevant than her chronological *age* for understanding how to guide her musical development. Nevertheless, ideally, a child will have passed through the acculturation type of preparatory audiation no later than when she turns four years old, through the imitation type of preparatory audiation no later than when she turns five years old, and through the assimilation type of preparatory audiation no later than when she turns six years old. Unfortunately, many children are not engaging in the imitation type of audiation at the time they enter school, and there are those children who enter school without ever having been guided through the acculturation type of preparatory audiation. Compensatory guidance

81

and instruction, of course, are possible, as is explained in Chapter Nine, for children with poor music backgrounds. On the other hand, there are children who enter the first stage of the assimilation type of preparatory audiation when they are as young as three years old, and there are children who enter the second stage of the assimilation type of preparatory audiation when they are as young as four years old. The quality of a child's early music experiences and her levels of developmental music aptitudes are the two most important factors that determine her current ability to engage in a given stage of preparatory audiation. That is true more for rhythm experiences and for rhythm aptitude than for tonal experiences and tonal aptitude. Rhythm is the fourth "R" which should be added to the three "R's." To the extent that her rhythm aptitude will allow, a child is what she feels. And, of course, to the extent that her tonal aptitude will allow, a child is what she hears.

Stage Six of Preparatory Audiation

The characteristic that distinguishes imitation from assimilation in preparatory audiation is that in imitation, the child is imitating what she hears in patterns or what she sees in movement without giving any more meaning to what she is doing than simply engaging in the act itself. The child is giving little, if any, syntactical meaning to what she is doing. It is like a child's imitating individual words when she is beginning to learn how to speak. Even if she knows what the individual words may mean, she probably is not thinking in phrases or sentences, nor is she giving syntactical meaning to the collection of words that she is speaking. Although the child is speaking, she may not be speaking with continuous comprehension. To perform patterns and to engage in body movement without assimilating them with each other in preparatory audiation is like speaking without assimilating what is being said with generalizations in summarized thought. A child cannot be taught assimilation. She must discover it for herself. That discovery is accomplished as a result of the child's being guided in absorbing musical sounds as she engages in the first five stages of preparatory audiation rather than as a result of her being formally taught to acquire music skills. If a child were to be taught formally to acquire music skills during the first five stages of preparatory audiation, it would be more detrimental to her music development than if no attention at all were paid to her music development during that time.

As in stage four of preparatory audiation, in stage six of preparatory audiation the child teaches herself. In both of those transition stages, the child is able to teach herself as a result of the appropriate guidance that the teacher or parent has provided and is providing. Without such guidance, the child probably would not proceed, if she were to move at all, to the seventh stage of preparatory audiation. Without stage seven of preparatory audiation as a readiness for audiation itself, the child would be limited in developing her audiation skills. The assimilation of the performance of patterns and of body and muscular movement is a prerequisite for effectively learning audiation skills.

Before guiding a child through the assimilation type of preparatory audiation, it is important to remember the distinctions between the different behaviors that are expected of the child, particularly in relation to tonal patterns and rhythm patterns, as the child phases through the three types of preparatory audiation. In the acculturation type of preparatory audiation, the child absorbs patterns. She does not imitate them, although she may attempt to do so. She enters the imitation type of preparatory audiation without first being able to imitate patterns in the acculturation type of preparatory audiation. In time she learns to imitate patterns with some precision in the imitation type of preparatory audiation. In the assimilation type of preparatory audiation, the child learns in time to perform patterns with some precision as she coordinates and assimilates the imitation of those patterns with the movement of her body and muscles.

In stage six of preparatory audiation, the child must not be told that the pattern that she is singing or chanting is not coordinated with the way she is moving. Nor should an attempt be made to instruct the child in how to coordinate the pattern that she is singing or chanting with the way she is moving. The child must discover for herself that the patterns that she is performing are not coordinated with the way she is moving. She must discover for herself the lack of assimilation. Without this realization which occurs at stage six of preparatory audiation, the child will not have the proper readiness to learn to coordinate the patterns with movement at stage seven of preparatory audiation. The tonal patterns and rhythm patterns that the child performs in stage six of preparatory audiation are the same as those that she performs in stages five and six of the imitation type of preparatory audiation.

The ability of a child to coordinate with herself naturally precedes the ability of the child to coordinate with someone else. Unless a child learns to coordinate with herself, she will not learn to coordinate with someone else. The distinction between those types of coordination must constantly be kept in mind by the teacher or parent who is guiding the child through both stages of the assimilation type of preparatory audiation. Particularly while the child is moving through the stages of preparatory audiation, the adult must remember that a child cannot learn to engage in more than one new activity at a time. To be able to engage in two activities, such as performing a pattern and moving at the same time, the child must be familiar with and capable of doing at least one of the activities.

It is possible that the child may not be aware of the relationship of her performance of patterns to her movement. Whether or not that is the case must be decided by the mature and experienced adult. If an attempt is made to guide a child in the assimilation type of preparatory audiation when the child has not progressed through the imitation type of preparatory audiation, no great harm will be done. If the adult decides that the child is not ready to engage in stage six of preparatory audiation, the adult should continue to work with the child, adapting the instruction as if the child were engaged in stage four or five of the imitation type of preparatory audiation. The decision to move a child back to an earlier stage of preparatory audiation should not be made in haste. Problems are more likely to arise if a child is returned to an earlier stage of preparatory audiation when it is not warranted than if a child is not returned to an earlier stage of preparatory audiation when it is warranted. Only time is lost in the latter case. Time is also lost, but more importantly, undesirable confusion is created in the mind of the child in the former case.

When the child has had sufficient experience in imitating tonal patterns and rhythm patterns and in moving with continuous motion in the imitation type of preparatory audiation, she is ready to enter stage six of preparatory audiation and to engage in movement activity which requires the ability to sustain movement while at the same time pulsating micro beats. Such movement activity is characterized by the child continuously moving with one or more parts of her body while at the same time she is using her arms, hands, legs, or feet, or any combination of those parts of her body, to pulsate micro beats. The child should begin such movement activity by sitting or standing in place and by emphasizing the use of the upper part of her body.

84

Only through sustained continuous movement can the consistent placement of micro beats be understood by the child. Time and space are best understood as they relate to sustained continuous movement. Perhaps the most important outcome of sustained continuous movement is that the child naturally accommodates her breathing to her movement. Unless movement and breathing comfortably interact in terms of weight and flow, the child will inadvertently rush and slow time and improperly estimate space when she performs micro beats in stage six of preparatory audiation and macro beats in stage seven of preparatory audiation. Rather than displacing her energy in breathing, the child who has not learned to subordinate her breathing to her movement will displace her energy by rushing, and sometimes by slowing, the speed of micro beats and macro beats. Weight and flow are child centered in terms of sustained movement, whereas time and space are adult centered in terms of discrete movement.

As soon as the child demonstrates that she is capable of engaging in sustained continuous movement as she sings tonal patterns and chants rhythm patterns, she should be directed to discontinue singing tonal patterns or chanting rhythm patterns as she is moving. Then, as she is engaging in sustained continuous movement, she should pulsate micro beats at the same tempo in which the teacher, using the syllable "bah," is chanting macro beats. Specifically, *in conjunction with sustained continuous movement and without performing patterns*, the child should pulsate two micro beats for every macro beat that the teacher chants. The child should not be encouraged to chant macro beats or micro beats (or patterns) as she is pulsating micro beats. Rather, she should pulsate micro beats using one or more parts of her body, as she chooses, continuously using the same body part over and over again, or randomly using different body parts to pulsate different micro beats. When different parts of the body are used in alternation, the movement to be discontinued must be continued until the new movement is underway. The child's pulsating of micro beats must not be in terms of staccato (separated) movements. That is, movement must not momentarily cease between pulsating micro beats.

When the child is able to pulsate micro beats as she is continuously moving, the teacher or parent no longer chants the syllable "bah" as the child is performing. Rather, the teacher chants some of the rhythm patterns suggested for use with the imitation type of preparatory audiation. The child should be directed to chant rhythm patterns after the adult has performed them as she, the child, is continuously moving and pulsating micro beats. The rhythm patterns should include four underlying macro beats. The child should not be directed to pulsate micro beats in conjunction with continuous movement as she is singing tonal patterns. Should she attempt to do so spontaneously, she should be discouraged from engaging in that activity.

The child's combining continuous sustained movement and pulsated micro beats as she chants rhythm patterns is best accomplished when the teacher or parent performs a chant without words or performs continuous macro beats with a neutral syllable, such as "bah." The use of words tends to reduce the child's predilection to attend to movement. Although a child who is phasing through the preparatory audiation stages is more concerned with tempo (in terms of micro beats) and repetitive patterns than she is with meter, because of their familiarity to her the child is compelled to pay more attention to words when they are used rather than to the tempo, meter, and rhythm of the music that is being performed.

Although the teacher or parent performs *macro* beats, the child pulsates *micro* beats. The tempo of the macro beats that the teacher or parent is performing should be faster than the tempo that is typically preferred by an adult. Because children have shorter arms and legs than adults, they prefer faster tempos. As a result of preferring faster tempos, children respond more comfortably to micro beats than to macro beats. When the child is emphasizing the use of her arms, the tempo should be faster than when she is emphasizing the use of her legs. Regardless of whether the teacher or parent is performing a chant or macro beats, the child should be guided in maintaining continuous movement even though the parent or teacher may include rests in the performance of the chant or macro beats. The use of recordings, play actions, and dramatizations of stories is not recommended when guiding children through learning sequence activities in either stage six or stage seven of the assimilation type of preparatory audiation.

After the child is comfortable in pulsating micro beats as she is moving continuously with sustained flexibility, she should be asked to chant rhythm patterns (*never tonal patterns*) as she is engaging in such movement. As soon as the child becomes aware that the rhythm patterns that she is performing are not coordinated with the way she is moving, she should be encouraged to enter the seventh and final stage of preparatory audiation. Such awareness typically becomes immediately obvious to the adult through the child's facial expressions.

Stage Seven of Preparatory Audiation

Different types of movement are undertaken as the child performs rhythm patterns and as the child performs tonal patterns. It is recommended that a child be guided in coordinating her chanting of rhythm patterns with movement before she is guided in coordinating her singing of tonal patterns with movement. First, techniques for assisting the child in coordinating movement and the chanting of rhythm patterns are presented. Next, the techniques for assisting the child in coordinating movement and the singing of tonal patterns are presented. Although the use of appropriate techniques by the teacher or parent is important in all types and at all stages of preparatory audiation, appropriate techniques become vitally important in the seventh stage of the assimilation type of preparatory audiation.

It is best to guide a child in coordinating her chanting of rhythm patterns with movement by first offering her help in movement alone, and then by helping her to chant rhythm patterns as she moves. Perhaps the most effective way of helping a child to pulsate micro beats while she is engaging in continuous sustained movement is through the use of the tongue. As the child is engaging in continuous sustained movement and in pulsating micro beats, she should say "ta" as she pulsates micro beats. A "ta" should be articulated at the same time and every time that a micro beat is pulsated; the articulation of every "ta" should be coordinated with the pulsation of every micro beat. Because the normal child initially finds it easier to move her tongue rather than any other part of her body with precision, she is able to use the tongue to direct the movement of other parts of her body with precision.

The child may become confused by the teacher's or parent's chanting macro beats with the syllable "bah" as she is chanting micro beats with the syllable "ta." When that is the case it is because of the different syllables rather than the different beats that are being performed. The teacher or parent should not attempt to remedy the situation by chanting the syllable "ta" rather than "bah," or by chanting micro beats rather than macro beats. In time the child will learn to attend to what she should be doing, and will no longer find that what the teacher or parent is chanting interferes with what she is chanting and doing. As a result of her performing and chanting one syllable while the teacher or parent is chanting another, the child will acquire the necessary readiness to engage in more complex aspects of stage seven of preparatory audiation, particularly when she ceases to chant only micro beats and begins to chant rhythm patterns. She ultimately will be engaging in continuous sustained movement, pulsating micro beats, and chanting rhythm patterns at the same time. When the child is capable of doing something different from what the adult is doing, she has established the readiness to move first to micro beats and then to macro beats without pulsating either micro beats or micro beats in a prescribed manner as she chants rhythm patterns. She will have internalized the feeling of the movement of micro beats and macro beats.

The ability to move is a necessary readiness for learning to be rhythmical. To adequately serve as a readiness for learning rhythm, movement must be of the continuous sustained type. For movement truly to be continuous and sustained, the child must emphasize weight and flow in movement before she attends to time and space in movement. Whereas the adult concentrates on giving precision to time and space in all types of movement, and perhaps never considers weight and flow, the young child intuitively and initially addresses herself to weight and flow as she engages in any type of movement. Guided to follow her natural inclination, and not being forced either beforehand, or even worse, at the same time, to engage consciously in time and space in terms of movement, a child will develop the necessary readiness to acquire appropriate rhythm skills and to develop musicianship in its broadest sense. Without a sense of weight in continuous sustained movement, the child will not appropriately learn to hop or to jump. Unless a child learns how to jump with proper preparation, preparation that a single hop on one or both feet cannot provide, she will not be able to begin to perform a song or a chant at the appropriate time, particularly if it begins with an upbeat. Neither will she be able to maintain a consistent tempo or to sustain a meter without assistance from someone else. Weight and flow in movement are not only fundamental for developing rhythm skills, they also are fundamental for developing singing skills and overall musicianship.

How the child breathes as well as how she moves is important particularly in the assimilation type of preparatory audiation, both tonally and rhythmically. The child needs to learn to coordinate naturally her breathing with her movement. Tonally, the emphasis is on vocal fold movement (covert movement) in conjunction with breathing. Rhythmically, the emphasis is on torso, arm, hand, foot, and leg movement (overt movement). Though it may seem contradictory, *in rhythm, movement is initiated by and is an outgrowth of breathing; in singing, breathing is initiated by and is an outgrowth of movement.*

The ability of the child intuitively to use the free and natural light weight of her body in continuous movement and to use her tongue in terms of bound flow will prove to be of help to her in learning how at the same time to pulsate micro beats in a consistent tempo. For a child who does not yet have that ability, one or more of the following techniques may be used. When employing any of the compensatory techniques, the child should not be encouraged to pulsate micro beats with any part or parts of her body at the same time that she is engaging in continuous movement, nor should she be encouraged to use her tongue to chant "ta" to micro beats. When she is able to pulsate micro beats in a consistent tempo as she is engaging in continuous movement, she should be encouraged again to coordinate her chanting of "ta" with the pulsating of micro beats in a consistent tempo as she is engaging in continuous sustained movement. She should be directed to pulsate micro beats with upper parts of her body before pulsating micro beats with lower parts of her body. Also, she should engage in continuous movement while pulsating and chanting micro beats as she stands in the same place before she moves around the room. Moreover, she should perform micro beats in usual duple meter before performing micro beats in usual triple meter. In usual triple meter, the weight of the first of each successive set of three micro beats (each macro beat) necessitates a shift from one side of the body to the other.

The following are individual activities to help children develop the ability to use weight in continuous sustained movement.
1. Coordination of hand movement:
    a. The children move both hands at the same time to the same place on each side of their bodies; for example, their left hands move to their left hips as their right hands move to their right hips.
    b. The children move one hand at a time to the same place on each side of their bodies; for example, their right hands move to their right knees and their left hands move to their left knees.

c. The children move one hand at a time to different places on opposite sides of their bodies; for example, their right hands move to their right knees and their left hands move to their left hips.

d. The children move both hands at the same time to different places on opposite sides of their bodies; for example, their right hands move to their right ears as their left hands move to the left side of their backs.

2. The teacher or parent and the child sit on the floor facing each other. They hold both of each other's hands and continually rock back and forth together.

3. The teacher or parent and the child sit on the floor facing each other. The palm of the adult's left hand touches the palm of the child's left hand and the palm of the adult's right hand touches the palm of the child's right hand as the arms move in circular motion.

4. The teacher or parent and the child sit on the floor facing each other. A ball should be cupped and *rolled underhand*, not thrown or bounced overhand, back and forth using both hands on the ball.

5. Demonstrate and model each activity by comparing it to another activity, in terms of same and different, keeping in mind that the appropriate speed of the movement for the child should feel somewhat fast for the adult.

6. The teacher or parent sits or kneels on the floor. The child stands and, with her hands on the adult's shoulders, pushes the adult's back forward. The adult than pushes her back to its original position. The motion should be smooth and continuous, with the child's hands remaining on the adult's shoulders.

7. As the children remain in the same place, they are directed to explore their personal space by continuously moving their arms, hands, legs, feet, and heads in all directions.

8. As the children remain in the same place, they are directed to use the natural weight associated with their body movement as they pulsate macro beats and continuously

a. rock from leg to leg while standing.

b. bend and straighten both knees while standing.

c. rock from leg to leg and bend one knee at a time while standing.

    d. rock from leg to leg and bend one knee at a time at the
       same time pivoting on the ball of the foot with the bent
       knee while standing.
    e. resting on one hip and then the other while standing.
    f. resting on one hip and then the other while kneeling.
    g. hopping.
    h. jumping.

Unless children take advantage of the value of the natural weight of their bodies, they will not achieve relaxed freedom in the flow of movement, which is fundamental for audiating and maintaining a consistent tempo. Natural weight should be used with various parts of the body, particularly the hips, legs, and arms. The more parts of the body that children move with natural weight, the sooner they will learn to pulsate micro beats in a consistent tempo. The children's ability to use natural weight with one part of their bodies does not mean necessarily that they will be able to use natural weight with another part, but they will learn. It may be suggested to the children often that they should feel that they are letting the rhythm out of their bodies rather than "pushing" it in.

    The following are group activities to help children develop the feeling of weight in continuous sustained movement.

   9. As children stand in a circle, each with both hands holding a
     hoop in the air, the hoop is moved back and forth and then up
     and down by the group at as much of a distance that their
     arms will allow.

 10. As children stand in a circle holding hands, they walk
     forward and close the circle and then walk backward and
     open the circle again, repeating the activity several times.
     The backward motion is the more important of the two.

 11. As children sit on the floor in a circle, they roll, throw, and
     bounce balls or bean bags back and forth. The entire arm,
     supported by natural weight, should be used to put the ball or
     bean bag in motion.

 12. Standing in two lines which face each other, the children,
     using both hands, pull on opposite sides of a rope. The rope
     is pulled back and forth without pauses, each group relaxing
     their hold on the rope and breathing deeply as the other group
     is pulling.

    After the child has demonstrated that she can move continuously while pulsating micro beats, without using her tongue to chant the syllable "ta," she can begin to chant rhythm patterns at the same time that she is moving continuously and pulsating micro beats, and she should begin to sing tonal patterns at the same time that she is moving continuously *without pulsating micro beats*. The tongue will, of course, be used to chant rhythm patterns and to sing tonal patterns. It will have been discovered that the child is more comfortable with and responds to rhythm activities more easily in the early stages of preparatory audiation. In later stages, she will respond to tonal activities just as easily.

If a child finds it difficult to perform tonal patterns and to engage in continuous sustained movement at the same time in stage seven of preparatory audiation, she should not be asked to perform tonal patterns without continuous sustained movement as she did in stage five of preparatory audiation. Such repetition in terms of overlearning will only postpone her musical development, and may even retard it. For the child who needs more assistance in learning how to coordinate her singing of tonal patterns with her movement, it will prove to be beneficial for her to prepare the singing of tonal patterns with a type of movement that is not totally continuous or sustained. Specifically, the child might hop or jump and then take a deep breath before she sings a tonal pattern, and then immediately engage in continuous movement as she is singing the tonal pattern. The same procedure should be followed for singing each pattern in a series of tonal patterns, allowing a short interval of time between the tonal patterns. It is important for the child to use the natural weight and flow of her body, particularly in the preparatory movement. The use of the natural weight and flow of her body must be sustained in movement as she is singing each tonal pattern. Also, before she is asked to sing tonal patterns as she is engaging in continuous sustained movement, she may be asked to sing only the resting tone in response to the teacher's or adult's singing the dominant pitch (for example, "SO" in major tonality or "MI" in minor tonality) as she is engaging in continuous sustained movement. The teacher or adult should sing the resting tone for, not with, the child, before the child is asked to sing the resting tone. When the child is successful in that activity, she may then be asked to sing complete tonal patterns, first those containing two pitches and then those containing three and four pitches, all the while engaging in continuous sustained movement.

When teaching children in a group at stage seven of preparatory audiation, the teacher should direct her attention to the idiographic individual musical characteristics of every child. Some children will have higher developmental tonal aptitudes than others. Some will have higher

audiation experiences. Whichever the case, the child will endure musical disadvantages as a result of such beliefs and actions by teachers and parents. The musical disadvantages to the child may prove to be so severe that he will make little musical progress, though he may develop some musical techniques and may learn how to deal with music notation. It is realistic to assume that under such conditions the child typically will probably develop negative attitudes toward music.

Children cannot realistically profit from formal instruction in music unless they have been guided through music babble. Music babble is associated with the first four stages of preparatory audiation. The transition from music babble to cultural musicianship is associated with the final three stages of preparatory audiation, while cultural musicianship is associated with all six stages of audiation. Before formal music instruction is given to children in or out of school, the extent to which they have had the benefit of unstructured and structured informal guidance in music must be diagnostically determined. Many of them will be discovered to have had some and even sufficient exposure to the first and second stages, and perhaps even the third stage, of the acculturation type of preparatory audiation. However, many of them will not have had any, let alone enough, exposure to the first or second stages of the imitation type of preparatory audiation or to the first and second stages of the assimilation type of audiation. Therefore, unstructured and structured informal guidance in music in school or in the home must be undertaken with those children at least in terms of imitation and assimilation before they are given formal instruction in music in or out of school. Although their degree of acculturation may be sufficient for them to engage immediately in imitation and assimilation, they will continually require additional acculturation to maintain and sustain their musical growth. Thus acculturation must always be present in the music education of students whether they are attending to music in terms of preparatory audiation or in terms of audiation itself. Children never outgrow their need to hear music in ways that are associated with the first three stages of the acculturation type of preparatory audiation.

Consider the following possible conditions that may be found in a class of children entering kindergarten or first grade. 1) The children have not yet found their singing voices, 2) the children have found their singing voices but they cannot imitate tonal patterns, 3) the children cannot move with sustained motion, 4) the children can move with sustained motion but they cannot at the same time pulsate micro beats, 5) the children can move simultaneously with sustained motion and pulsate micro beats but they cannot at the same time chant rhythm patterns. When one or more of those conditions, or similar types of conditions, are discovered, the children must be given unstructured and structured informal guidance in the appropriate type or types and stage or stages of preparatory audiation to compensate for one or more of their deficiencies before formal instruction in music is begun. Depending upon the number of children that have deficiencies in music, part of a class period or an entire class period may need to be devoted to remedial work. Although many school administrators believe that all children should be given formal instruction in music when they are of school age, it is much more reasonable to assume that class time will need to be allotted to giving at least some children unstructured and structured informal guidance in music. It may take one semester or one academic year of exposure to preparatory audiation before children have acquired the necessary readiness for formal instruction in music.

Ideally, children will have had the benefit of unstructured and structured informal guidance in music, including all three types and seven stages of preparatory audiation, before they enter school. In such a situation, formal instruction may be confidently begun. It is recommended that at that time, *Jump Right In: The Music Curriculum* (Gordon and Woods, 1986) be used. That curriculum includes both learning sequence activities and classroom activities. The learning sequence activities represent a natural and sequential transition from unstructured and structured informal guidance in music, in terms of preparatory audiation, to formal instruction in music, in terms of audiation. Discrimination is the readiness for recognition. Recognition is the readiness for imitation. Imitation is the readiness for audiation. An important distinction between preparatory audiation and audiation is that while passing through the types and stages of preparatory audiation, a child's potential for learning how to audiate is enhanced. While passing through the types and stages of audiation, a child learns *what* to audiate as he continues to learn how to audiate.

When all children in a kindergarten or first grade class have been successfully phased through unstructured and structured informal guidance in music, formal instruction in music in terms of learning sequence activities is typically initiated with Tonal Unit 1, Section A, Criterion 1 and with Rhythm Unit 1, Section A, Criteria 1 of *Jump Right In: The Music Curriculum*. Whether or not the children who have

96

successfully been phased through unstructured and structured informal guidance in music are older than five or six years of age, and even if they are in the upper grades, formal instruction in music in terms of learning sequence activities typically begins with Tonal Unit 1, Section A, Criterion 1 and with Rhythm Unit 1, Section A, Criteria 1. There is always the possibility that some children will have emerged from informal guidance and stage seven of preparatory audiation and will have been introduced to formal instruction and audiation before they enter school. They may have been taught some aspects of *Jump Right In: The Music Curriculum* in preschool. When most of the children in a class fit that description, a teacher may decide that formal instruction in music might begin with more advanced criteria, sections, or units of *Jump Right In: The Music Curriculum.*

The full edition of *Jump Right In: The Music Curriculum* is designed so that Criteria 1 and 2 of Sections A and B of Tonal Unit 1 and Criteria 1 and 2 of Sections A and B of Rhythm Unit 1 learning sequence activities serve as transitions between preparatory audiation and audiation. They are transitions in the sense that they reinforce skills that were taught to children in the imitation and assimilation types of preparatory audiation. In Criterion 1 of Section A of Tonal Unit 1, children are asked to sing only the first pitch of a tonal pattern in major tonality that the teacher has sung. In Criterion 2 of Section A of Tonal Unit 1, children are asked to sing only the resting tone of the tonality of the tonal pattern in major tonality that the teacher has sung. Beginning with Criterion 3, Section A of Tonal Unit 1, children are introduced to and asked to sing, using a neutral syllable, entire tonic and dominant arpeggioed tonal patterns in major tonality, most of which are more complex than those that were presented to them in preparatory audiation. They will then be introduced to and asked to sing arpeggioed tonal patterns in other functions, such as subdominant. The same procedure is followed in Criteria 1, 2, and 3 in Section B of Tonal Unit 1 with tonal patterns in minor tonality. Beginning with Criterion 1, Section A of Tonal Unit 2, children are asked to sing tonal patterns, using tonal syllables as they audiate objective tonality. As in informal guidance, in formal instruction tonal patterns are sung without rhythm. However, unlike informal guidance, children are asked to sing tonal patterns in solo as well as in ensemble. Without solo singing, a child will be unable to develop audiation skills. With the exception of some levels of skill learning sequence, though never the aural/oral or verbal association levels, the tonality and keyality in which the tonal patterns are to be

97

performed in learning sequence activities are always established in a special way for the children immediately before they begin to sing.

The relationship of the functions of patterns to learning sequence activities in formal instruction is complex. Easy patterns are taught to children before more difficult ones. Nonetheless, although subdominant function patterns, as a group, are easier for children to audiate than either tonic function patterns as a group or dominant function patterns as a group, the latter two functions must be taught before the former in major and minor tonalities. Unless that sequence is followed, the children's development of a sense of major tonality and minor tonality will at best be delayed and at worst distorted. Perhaps the reason lies in the absence of the leading tone in subdominant function patterns. That hypothesis becomes more plausible when it is remembered that children engaging in preparatory audiation find the single dominant pitch easier than the single tonic pitch both to audiate and to perform in major tonality and minor tonality.

It is not advisable to suggest to children when they are learning the arpeggioed tonal patterns that they attempt to hear silently the diatonic pitches between the arpeggioed pitches. Such an effort wastes time, because it does not enhance the audiation of arpeggioed tonal patterns. In fact, children may be led to think that all tonal patterns are variations of one essential tonal pattern, perhaps a scale, not realizing that each tonal pattern is audiated in a unique manner. Consider the consequences if children were taught to respond to the word "cat" by being made aware of and told to think of the "missing b" between the first two letters of the word.

In Criterion 1 of Section A of Rhythm Unit 1 of the full edition of *Jump Right In: The Music Curriculum*, children are asked to move informally with continuous sustained movement, and, if the teacher desires, at the same time with pulsating micro beats, without chanting, as the teacher chants macro beats and micro beats in usual duple meter. In Criterion 2 of Section A of Rhythm Unit 1, children are asked to move their legs in a prescribed manner to macro beats as the teacher chants macro beats. When children are engaging in the assimilation type of preparatory audiation, they move to micro beats without moving to macro beats, and they move to macro beats without moving to micro beats. In Criterion 3 of Section A of Rhythm Unit 1, however, children are asked to move their arms to micro beats at the same time that they are moving their legs to macro beats as the teacher chants macro beats and micro beats in usual duple meter. The same procedure is followed in Criteria 1, 2, and 3 in Section B of Rhythm Unit 1 with macro beats and micro beats in usual triple meter. In the two remaining sections of Rhythm Units 1 and 2, children are asked at first to chant macro and micro beat rhythm patterns using a neutral syllable without moving to macro beats and micro beats. Later they are asked to chant the patterns as they are moving arms, hands, feet, and legs to macro beats and micro beats. Beginning with Criterion 1, Section A of Rhythm Unit 2, children are asked to chant rhythm patterns, using rhythm syllables as they audiate using their bodies but not moving in a prescribed manner to macro beats or micro beats in an objective meter. As in informal guidance, in formal instruction all durations in a rhythm pattern are chanted on the same pitch and are performed with expressive inflection. However, unlike informal guidance, in formal instruction children are asked to chant rhythm patterns in solo as well as in ensemble. Without solo chanting, a child will be unable to develop audiation skills. With the exception of some levels of skill learning sequence, though never the aural/oral and verbal association levels, the tempo and meter in which the rhythm patterns are to be performed in learning sequence activities is always established in a special way for the children immediately before they begin to chant.

The differences in the way children respond to music when they are engaging in preparatory audiation and when they are engaging in audiation becomes increasingly evident. Nonetheless, it is easy to confuse learning sequence activities as they apply to preparatory audiation and audiation. When such confusion occurs, specifically when it is *incorrectly* assumed that the stages and types of preparatory audiation and audiation are not in correspondence and one must be changed, learning becomes impaired. In preparatory audiation activities, children 1) must perform micro beats alone before they perform macro beats alone, and 2) must not perform macro beats and micro beats at the same time. Whereas in audiation activities, children 1) must perform macro beats alone, before they perform micro beats alone and 2) they must perform macro beats and micro beats at the same time before they perform micro beats alone. Thus it is with good reason that in Sections A and B of Rhythm Unit 1 of the full edition of *Jump Right In: The Music Curriculum*, children are asked to move to macro beats alone in Criterion 2 and then to macro beats and micro beats at the same time in Criterion 3. It is not until Criterion 3 of Sections C and D of Rhythm Unit 1 that children are asked to move to micro beats alone. To alter the sequence of either of those units or of those Criteria would be to prevent children from receiving appropriate sequential instruction in developing coordination and a sense of consistency of tempo.

The tonal and rhythm transitions from preparatory audiation to audiation are similar in the full edition and the revised edition of *Jump Right In: The Music Curriculum*. With particular regard to the rhythm transition, in the initial criteria of the revised edition, the child is immediately directed to move to macro beats and to micro beats at the same time that he is chanting rhythm patterns. If the student is not capable of such activities, the types of movement learned in preparatory audiation are either taught or reviewed by the teacher through the use of *Jump Right In: The Early Childhood Music Curriculum*.

As explained elsewhere (Gordon, 1989), there are three music learning theories that are given practical application in learning sequence activities. All three are associated with formal instruction in music. They are skill learning theory, tonal content learning theory, and rhythm content learning theory. Skill learning sequence activities must be combined with either tonal content learning sequence activities or rhythm content learning sequence activities. In terms of music learning theory in formal instruction in music, tonal patterns and rhythm patterns, in conjunction with discrimination skills and inference skills, are emphasized in learning sequence activities, whereas the performance of music literature is emphasized in classroom activities. Also, in formal instruction, tonalities and meters (content) are introduced in classroom activities and tonal patterns and rhythm patterns, in conjunction with the levels of discrimination learning and inference learning (skills), are introduced in learning sequence activities. Learning sequence activities and classroom activities are designed to be combined in the educational setting so that they reinforce each other. When no provision is made for learning sequence activities and only classroom activities are used in formal instruction, recreation, notation, and music theory may feed upon one another to meet the short term goals of maintaining classroom discipline and promoting a "good" attitude toward music. However, as a result, long range goals are sacrificed.

In preparatory audiation, the child is concerned with subjective tonalities and meters. In audiation, the teacher or parent is, and in time the child will be, concerned with objective tonalities and meters. Only major and minor tonalities and usual duple and triple meters are performed by the teacher for children engaging in preparatory audiation activities to assist them in making the transition from an understanding of subjective tonality and meter to an understanding of objective tonality and meter. In addition to major and harmonic minor, other tonalities, such as mixolydian and dorian, are performed by the teacher for children who are engaging in audiation activities to assist them in developing an understanding of objective tonalities. In addition to usual duple and usual triple, other meters, such as usual combined and unusual paired, are performed by the teacher for children who are engaging in audiation activities to assist them in developing an understanding of objective meters.

Because many music teachers do not understand music learning theory, they attempt to teach what they consider to be audiation in association with discrimination learning, and they attempt to teach the reading of notation in association with inference learning. To do so is to violate the basic tenets of music learning theory. When taught correctly, children intuitively learn to recall patterns through syntactical audiation. When taught incorrectly, they learn to memorize individual pitches through some type of imitation. In formal instruction in music, children should acquire large listening and performing vocabularies of tonal patterns and rhythm patterns. Then, as a result of their exposure to various tonalities and meters, children learn to audiate patterns syntactically. As a result of developing tonal pattern and rhythm pattern vocabularies in different tonalities and meters at the aural/oral and verbal association levels of learning, children acquire the readiness to develop additional skills, such as synthesizing, reading, writing, creating, and improvising in terms of discrimination and inference learning, at higher levels of music learning theory. As children sequentially learn more and more patterns, they are better able to develop music syntax in terms of objective tonality and meter, and as children develop a sense of objective tonality and a sense of objective meter, they are better able to learn more and more patterns.

In learning language, children learn to listen and speak and then they learn to read and write. They are not taught reading skills before they can listen and speak with comprehension. Children should also learn to listen and to perform music with comprehension before they are taught music reading skills. If reading skills are taught before comprehension, facts, not function, are taught, and students simply learn the names of the

101

lines and spaces of the staff and the time values of notes. It is like seeing and memorizing the alphabet and not understanding words. Learning to read with comprehension is more a matter of *what* than *how*. The syntactic imitation and then the audiation of patterns is just as important for learning how to create and improvise music as it is for learning how to read and write music notation. A teacher cannot teach a child creativity and improvisation. A teacher can only provide a child with the readiness to teach himself how to create and to improvise. Learning is the residual of teaching.

In formal instruction in music, the reading of notation is taught before the writing of notation at the symbolic association, composite synthesis, and appropriate inference levels of skill learning theory. Whereas, because children comprehend language, it is possible to teach them writing before reading as well as reading before writing; that is not the case in music. Typically children enter school without a sufficient listening or performing vocabulary of tonal patterns or rhythm patterns. Therefore, they lack the ability to write as a result of not being able to comprehend through audiation something to write about. They cannot even write patterns from dictation, let alone patterns that they create themselves. Because their listening and performing vocabularies of tonal patterns and rhythm patterns are small, as compared to their linguistic listening and speaking vocabularies, children necessarily need to learn how to read patterns that they can audiate before they can write them with comprehension.

Unlike the procedure followed when children are engaging in preparatory audiation, the sequence followed in audiation for the teaching of tonal patterns and rhythm patterns is based upon the experimentally established difficulty levels of these patterns. Easy patterns are taught before moderately difficult patterns, and moderately difficult patterns are taught before difficult patterns. In teaching, it is easy to make things difficult but it is difficult to make things easy. When patterns are taught sequentially in learning sequence activities according to their difficulty levels, difficult patterns are made easy. When patterns are taught according to the frequency with which they are found in the literature that is used in classroom activities, or because they correspond to children's "speech rhythms," easy patterns are made difficult.

In formal instruction in music, children continue the practice followed in preparatory audiation of using neutral syllables to perform tonal patterns and rhythm patterns at the aural/oral level of skill learning sequence. They are taught to use tonal syllables and rhythm syllables, however, at the verbal association level of skill learning sequence. It is important that they use tonal solfege rather than numbers or the letter names of the lines and spaces of the staff. If they use numbers or letters, they become confused when, as is often the case, tonal patterns require that numbers or letters be skipped and used backward. It is also important that children use rhythm solfege rather than the time value names of notes or numbers as in counting. They become confused by numbers, even though they follow a logical order, because numbers bear a relationship to notation, not to audiation. Additional problems are encountered when numbers are used with both tonal patterns and rhythm patterns. To use numbers to learn instrumental fingerings further complicates matters. Also, the time value names of notes bear a relationship to notation, not to audiation. Because rhythm syllables are based upon beat functions, they bear a direct relationship to audiation. A detailed discussion and description of comparative tonal and rhythm systems of verbal association may be found in other sources (Gordon, 1989).

Though it may seem contradictory, in preparatory audiation children must be given the opportunity to respond to tonal and rhythm syntax before they can be expected to respond to tonal and rhythm patterns. However, in audiation, children are given the opportunity to respond to tonal and rhythm patterns before they are expected to respond to tonal and rhythm syntax. If an adult lacks an understanding of even that one difference in the way children sequentially learn music when they are engaging in preparatory audiation as compared to when they are engaging in audiation and if, as a result children are given formal instruction in music without first having the readiness that preparatory audiation provides, the consequences will be most unfortunate. When such readiness is not given consideration, children will need to spend an inordinate amount of time when they are older to unlearn what they were forced to learn when they were younger. They will need to unlearn in order to learn.

Singing and chanting are especially important components of classroom activities in formal instruction in music. The singing of songs and the chanting of chants in classroom activities introduce children to specific tonalities and meters as a readiness for teaching them to audiate tonal patterns and rhythm patterns in those tonalities and meters in

103

learning sequence activities. In order for children to enjoy singing and chanting and at the same time develop a sense of tonality and meter through the performance of songs and chants, the teacher or parent must teach the songs and chants in an appropriate manner. The songs and chants should be taught by rote, with the children as a group imitating the song or chant. No child should be asked to perform a song or chant in solo and no attempt should be made to teach the children to memorize either of them. As the children learn to audiate, they will be better able to learn songs and chants, as they should, through recall. It is best to teach songs and chants without words. If desired, words may added after the children are able to perform a song with a sense of tonality and acceptable intonation and to perform a chant with a sense of meter, in a consistent tempo, and with acceptable rhythm. Words are as distracting for children in vocal music as the letter names of the keys on a keyboard are in instrumental music.

When it is determined that some children have not yet found their singing voices, they must be given informal guidance in doing so. It must be remembered by the teacher or parent that a singing voice is a more a matter of quality than of range. Singing quality is characteristically lighter and more flexible than the speaking voice. There is an absence of tension, strain, and tightness in the sound. The throat feels open, and the tone flows with the breath. Correct singing quality may be used even though the pitches that are sung are in the speaking voice range. On the other hand, pitches may be produced well above the speaking voice range but still in speaking voice quality. With that type of voice production, the sound is strained, squeaky, and unmusical.

The simplest way to teach a child to find his singing voice is to have him breathe, produce a long and loud yell, which then (without a break) becomes a soft yell. When the child does that, he will produce a pitch near or between F-sharp and A above middle C. The initial singing range and natural audiation range of the beginning young singer or one with a changed voice is from D above middle C to A, a perfect fifth above. (The natural audiation range is one into which the child transposes what is heard outside that range in order to give sound musical meaning.) As soon as the child produces a pitch in the upper part of his initial singing range, the teacher should imitate his pitch. In time, perhaps in a few days, when the child's singing voice is stabilized, the child should engage in learning sequence activities so that he will begin to imitate the teacher's or parent's pitches as they occur in tonal patterns found in both the full and revised editions of *Jump Right In: The Music Curriculum*. In that way, the child will first learn to sing with a singing voice quality and then learn to sing with good intonation.

In the preparatory audiation stage, the adult sings for the child and rarely with the child. In the audiation stage, the adult usually sings both for and with the child. The child must engage first in ensemble singing and then in solo singing in formal instruction in order to learn how to audiate. The adult should keep in mind that when a child sings in solo, his voice sounds louder to him than when he is singing in unison with an adult or another child. As a result, when he first sings in solo, the child may think that something is wrong, because his voice sounds so different. The adult must guide the child in understanding that although his voice may sound different to him when singing under different conditions, that is to be expected. The better the young male child is able to sing with good intonation in solo, the easier it will be for him to learn how to use his changing and changed voice when he is older. If he does not learn to sing with good intonation before his voice begins to change, the chances are that he will not be able to learn to sing with good intonation after his voice has changed.

In order for a child to continue singing with good quality and intonation in learning sequence activities, techniques for teaching rote songs and chants in classroom activities must be designed. The goal may be best accomplished by establishing the tonality, keyality, beginning pitch, tempo, and meter of the song and establishing the tempo and meter of the chant before the children are asked to perform the song or chant. Good intonation is developed as a result of the child's being able to audiate the appropriate resting tone as each pitch in every tonal pattern of a song is performed. Likewise, good rhythm is developed as a result of the child's being able to audiate the appropriate macro beats and micro beats as each duration in every rhythm pattern of a song or chant is performed. The dynamics and style of a song or chant should be established for the children before they are asked to perform the song or chant.

When care is not taken in teaching rote songs and chants, the problems of a child with a poor sense of tonality and intonation or with a poor sense of meter and consistency of tempo increase. To promote the development of good tonal audiation when teaching tonal patterns in learning sequence activities or rote songs in classroom activities, the male teacher or parent should sing in a head voice, not falsetto, only one octave below what the children are singing. To promote the development of good rhythm audiation, chants and rote songs should first be taught without words. The pronunciation of a word when speaking is often different from the pronunciation of a word when singing or chanting. Words should not be used as mnemonic devices to teach rhythm. If words must be used and if they are taught separately, they should be chanted as they are found in the rhythm of the song or the chant. The tempo of a song or chant need not be slowed to teach words. If a mistake is made, it should not be assumed that the song or chant must be begun again at the beginning. That procedure fosters memorization rather than audiation. In language, if one is thinking, he does not need to go back to the beginning of a narration, or even to the beginning of a sentence if a word is not spoken correctly. In music, if one is audiating, he does not need to go back to the beginning of a song or chant or to the beginning of a phrase if a pattern is not performed correctly. For one who audiates, there are no mistakes; there are only wrong solutions. Detailed procedures for teaching songs and chants by rote may be found elsewhere (Gordon, 1989).

Neither in learning sequence activities in preparatory audiation nor in learning sequence activities in audiation do children perform tonal patterns in pentatonic. The reason is that pentatonic has no leading tone, and without the presence of a leading tone, a sense of tonality cannot be established. Without a sense of tonality, good intonation cannot be established. Major pentatonic, minor pentatonic, dorian pentatonic, and so on, exist only in notation, not in audiation. In learning sequence activities in formal instruction, tonal patterns are performed in distinct tonalities. Although the children are first asked to sing only arpeggioed tonal patterns and no diatonic tonal patterns in major and harmonic minor tonalities, they do sing the fourth and seventh steps of the scales which are the theoretical bases of those tonalities. Dominant function tonal patterns include the seventh step and subdominant function tonal patterns the fourth step. However, because pauses are made between the singing of tonal patterns in learning sequence activities, pitches separated by less than the interval of a third are at first not sung successively. Once children have developed a sense of tonality and are able to sing with good intonation, diatonic patterns are introduced in learning sequence activities. There is no reason, however, to avoid at any time the singing of pentatonic songs and patterns in classroom activities. It is advantageous to introduce songs in many different tonalities and meters and chants in many meters in classroom activities as soon as formal instruction in music is begun.

There are differences and similarities in the conditions under which a group of children are given unstructured and structured informal guidance in music and formal instruction in music. In unstructured and structured informal guidance, preferably there should be no more than twelve children in a group. There should always be a teacher and one or more assistant teachers present. Although one meeting a week produces desirable results, a group should meet twice a week if possible. The class periods should be approximately one half hour long. Learning sequence activities may be taught at any time during the class period. The children should be grouped according to their musical age rather than their chronological age. In formal instruction, ideally there should be no more than twenty-four children in a group. The class period should be no longer than forty minutes and no shorter than thirty minutes. A group should meet three times a week. Learning sequence activities should be taught during the first ten minutes of the class period. If a group meets four or five times a week, learning sequence activities should be taught only three times a week, preferably on alternate days. Classroom activities, of course, should be taught during every class period. If it is possible, the children should be grouped according to their musical ages rather than by grade according to their chronological ages.

During the first few weeks of school, no learning sequence activities should be taught. Classroom activities during those weeks should be used to acquaint the children with as many tonalities and meters as possible through their performance of songs and chants, particularly those without words. Also, because teaching to children's individual musical differences is so important in formal instruction in music, initial class periods must be used to administer either developmental or stabilized music aptitude tests to the children. Only when the teacher has children's test results, may formal instruction in music with the use of learning sequence activities be appropriately begun.

Once the teacher knows children's music aptitude scores, teaching may be adapted to their individual musical differences. That is best accomplished in learning sequence activities. (Enrichment and compensatory formal instruction in music may be profitably undertaken as well in classroom activities.) In learning sequence activities, each child is asked to perform in solo the easy pattern in a criterion. When children with average and high music aptitudes are able to perform in solo the easy pattern in the criterion, they are asked to perform in solo the moderately difficult pattern in the criterion; and at the same time, children with low music aptitude continue to learn to perform in solo the easy pattern in the criterion. When children with high music aptitude are able to perform in solo the moderately difficult pattern in the criterion, they are asked to perform in solo the difficult pattern in the criterion while children with average aptitude continue to learn to perform in solo the moderately difficult pattern, and children with low music aptitude continue to learn to perform in solo the easy pattern in the criterion.

The results of a music aptitude test are far more reliable and usually more valid than teacher's judgments about the music aptitudes of the children that they are teaching. Still, tests are by no means perfect. Therefore, even though a test score may indicate that a child's music aptitude is low or average, he must be given the opportunity to learn to perform moderately difficult or difficult patterns. Should a child be capable of performing at a level higher than his music aptitude test score might suggest, which is usually not the case, obviously the score is in error and instruction for the child should be adapted accordingly. Also, it should be anticipated that when a child is in the developmental music aptitude stage and is receiving appropriate instruction, particularly in learning sequence activities, his music aptitude should increase within the course of a semester or less. Unfortunately, with inappropriate instruction, developmental music aptitude test scores typically decrease as a child moves from grade to grade.

In formal instruction in learning sequence activities and classroom activities, monitoring a child's musical growth in terms of his music achievement is very important. Provision is made in both the full and revised editions of *Jump Right In: The Music Curriculum* for measuring and evaluating the extent to which each child is achieving at each level of skill learning sequence, tonal content learning sequence, and rhythm content learning sequence. Continual comparisons should be made between a child's potential to achieve in music (his music aptitude) and his actual achievement.

Chapter Nine

INSTRUMENTAL MUSIC

Many parents want their children to take lessons on music instruments at an early age. Some parents who have a child enrolled in a preschool music class decide that the child has so much "talent" that she should begin taking lessons on a music instrument. Some parents are convinced that the sooner a child begins to take lessons on a music instrument, the easier it will be for her to learn and the better she will learn to play. Other parents believe that the best way for a child to become musically acculturated is by taking lessons on a music instrument. More serious thought must be given to whether and when a child should to begin taking lessons on a music instrument.

There is no correct chronological age for a child to begin taking lessons on a music instrument. Far more important than the child's chronological age is her musical age. Certainly a child should have emerged from tonal babble and rhythm babble and have passed through most, preferably all, of the types and stages of preparatory audiation before she begins to take lessons on any music instrument. Unless a child can sing in tune and move her body with good rhythm, she will not be able to learn to play a music instrument in tune or with good rhythm. With the possible exception of a fixed pitch instrument such as the piano, music instruments do not inherently have good intonation. Nor does any music instrument inherently have good rhythm. Music instruments are extensions of the persons who perform on them. Unless a performer can audiate with a sense of tonality, a sense of meter, good intonation, a consistent tempo, and good rhythm, it cannot be expected that she will be able to learn to play a music instrument and demonstrate those attributes. Though there may be valves, keys, or frets on an instrument, it remains the performer's responsibility to constantly make adjustments in order to establish good intonation. With regard to rhythm, no ordinary music instrument has even the mechanical provision to assist in producing proper durations or meters. A detailed discussion of instrumental music may be found elsewhere (Gordon, 1989).

Although being able to audiate with a sense of tonality and a sense of meter are necessary readinesses for taking lessons on a music instrument, they are not sufficient. A child must have developed a singing vocabulary of tonal patterns in at least major tonality and minor tonality and a chanting vocabulary of rhythm patterns in at least usual duple meter and usual triple meter. Just as successful actors audiate words and not individual letters, so successful instrumentalists audiate patterns and not individual pitches or durations.

Instrumental music lessons can prove to be profitable for a child whether she is in the developmental music aptitude stage or in the stabilized music aptitude stage. A child who is three or four years old, although still in the developmental aptitude stage, may have the readiness to begin to take lessons on a music instrument because she has developed an objective sense of tonality and an objective sense of meter. Another child in middle school, although she is in the stabilized music aptitude stage, may not have the readiness to begin to take lessons on a music instrument because she has only a subjective sense of tonality and a subjective sense of meter.

There is a common belief that a child's physical characteristics should be given first consideration when choosing a music instrument for her to learn to play. Physical characteristics cannot be totally discounted. However, it is of far more importance to a child's achievement on a music instrument, as well as to her attitude toward continuing study, that she have a preference for the tone quality of the instrument. Many children choose a music instrument to play and many parents choose music instruments for their children to play for musically irrelevant reasons. Little regard is given to whether the child, and not necessarily the parent, has a preference for the tone quality of the instrument. Allowing a child to see or hear an actual music instrument often raises issues and concerns that override the comparative tone qualities of the instruments. A parent or teacher might better use an objective test of synthesized sounds for selecting a suitable music instrument for a child. The *Instrument Timbre Preference Test* (Gordon, 1984) may be used for identifying the most appropriate music instrument for a child either when she is just beginning to take lessons, or if she is dissatisfied with the instrument that she is playing.

Selecting a teacher for a child must be undertaken cautiously. A thoughtful and competent teacher understands the nature of instrumental music readiness and, if a child lacks such readiness, the teacher provides it as part of the instructional process. It may be necessary to guide a child through unstructured and/or structured informal guidance in preparatory audiation as she is taking lessons, or it may be necessary to teach the child to audiate and to sing tonal patterns and to audiate and to chant rhythm patterns at the aural/oral and verbal association levels of skill learning theory in terms of formal instruction during lessons. If remedial instruction is needed, whether of the preparatory audiation or audiation type, a lesson can be separated into listening, singing, chanting, and movement experiences on the one hand and instrumental experiences on the other. Both will necessarily include learning sequence activities as well as instrumental (classroom) activities. In group lessons, the two types of experiences may be taught alternately during the same lesson. That is not as easily accomplished in private lessons. When instrumental lessons are given to children privately, the children should meet at least once a week as a group. They should not play instruments at that time. They should sing, chant, and move in various tonalities and meters as they acquire listening and performing vocabularies of tonal patterns and rhythm patterns. As in formal instruction in classroom activities and learning sequence activities in school, it is not necessary to coordinate musical content, that is, tonalities, tonal patterns, meters, or rhythm patterns, with the literature that the children are performing with or without instruments.

A good teacher of instrumental music understands that a child must be taught two instruments. One is the actual instrument that the child is learning to play, such as a piano or a saxophone. It is visible. The other is the child's audiation instrument. It is invisible; it is inside of the child's head. A child must develop instrumental technique to play the actual instrument. However, unless she also develops audiation skills, regardless of how well she has developed instrumental technique, she will not learn to play the instrument in a musical manner. Technically manipulating an instrument without audiation is like speaking without thinking. Ideally, a child should begin lessons on an actual instrument after she has developed her audiation instrument. Achievement with the audiation instrument provides the readiness to learn to play the actual instrument. When there is no such readiness, the teacher must provide the readiness at least concurrently with, if not before, lessons on the actual instrument.

Before a child is given lessons on a music instrument, an appropriate developmental or stabilized music aptitude test should be administered to her. In that way, the teacher will best be able to adapt instruction in performance activities and learning sequence activities to her individual musical needs. That is true for both group and private lessons, but a teacher can best adapt learning sequence activities to a child's individual musical needs when the child is enrolled in group lessons. When children are being taught instrumental music as a group and there are various levels of music aptitudes represented in the group, each child can sing, chant, and perform on a music instrument tonal patterns and rhythm patterns that are easy, moderately difficult, or difficult, depending upon her levels of tonal and rhythm aptitudes. When special group classes are held for children who study privately, teaching to their individual musical needs through learning sequence activities is of particular importance.

Children taking lessons on music instruments should be grouped heterogeneously in terms of music aptitude. Also, all children should not be playing the same kind of instrument. It is of more value to have children playing instruments from different families of instruments, such as brass and woodwind, than to have all of them playing instruments from one family. When a child has to listen to the timbres of various types of instruments which are producing various pitches and at the same time she has to adjust her intonation and rhythm to the sounds of the group as a whole, her audiation skills develop more rapidly as a result of her needing to adapt her audiation to practical demands.

The regimen associated with learning to play a music instrument is typically based upon the amount of time that a child practices. That is unfortunate. If a child is audiating what she intends to play, she can benefit more from short practice periods than a child who is not audiating can benefit from long practice periods. The shorter the practice time and the more times that a child practices, the more she will learn. The longer the practice time and the fewer times that a child practices, the less she will learn. Much can be learned away from an instrument if a child is able to audiate what she has practiced or what she intends to practice. One responsibility of a teacher is to teach a child how to practice, not to praise or scold a child by keeping a record of how long and how many times she has practiced. Children who can audiate will soon become self directed in what, when, and how long to practice.

When taking lessons, when practicing, and when performing in solo and ensemble in public, many children unfortunately develop unnecessary tension. Though some tension is always present when one is performing, unnecessary tension can become debilitating. The primary reason for tension is not nervousness. Rather, tension occurs because a child is unsure of the sound of what she is supposed to be playing. Many children are taught to imitate and to memorize for a recital what they have heard their teacher play. Others memorize from notation what they are to perform in recital. Anxiety and tension are normal responses in situations where a child is unable to audiate and must rely on imitation and memorization. If a child is capable of engaging in audiation, she can easily recall what it is that she is to play and can free herself from tension.

Tension is often associated with technical difficulties in playing an instrument. There is reason to believe that problems which a child encounters in instrumental technique, problems of fingering and embouchure, for example, are not really technical problems. They are audiation problems. (Audiation problems are the result of a child's lack of ability to sing tonal patterns and to chant rhythm patterns in more than one objective tonality and in more than one objective meter.) That is, most technical problems are caused by the child's inability to audiate what she is attempting to play on an instrument. When the child is audiating, embouchure on a wind instrument and fingers on a stringed instrument become pitch selectors, and movements of the body become duration selectors. Technical problems on an instrument have their source in audiation problems. Audiation problems do not have their source in instrumental technique problems. On the contrary, good audiation skills tend to prevent and correct instrumental technique problems.

Audiation is necessary for proper breathing when one is playing a music instrument as well as when one is singing and moving. When a child audiates what she is going to play on an instrument before she plays it, she takes in the correct amount of breath as she is audiating. Thus she does not run out of breath before the end of a phrase, nor does she have a residue of breath after the phrase has been played. Preparing for and using the correct amount of breath when playing an instrument are important for playing that instrument musically.

The types of movements one makes should direct the manner in which one breathes. In playing a music instrument, however, the way one breathes should direct the types of movements one makes. When singing, chanting, and playing a music instrument, the way one breathes is of great importance for performing in a musical manner. Breathing should be continuous, that is, without unnecessary pauses. The stopping of air between durations in a rhythm pattern is not the same as pauses between breaths. Improper movement has a tendency to interfere with continuous breathing in workaday activities as well as in performing on an instrument or with the voice. Unless a child is audiating, the chances are that her breathing will not be continuous, and that she will experience unnecessary tension when playing a music instrument or singing.

The teacher should consider both inhaling and exhaling when teaching a child how to sing, to chant, and to play a music instrument. Audiation should be emphasized when one is inhaling. The performance of what was audiated should be emphasized when one is exhaling. The consequences of not audiating have been explained. However, the consequences seem to be as severe when a child attempts to technically execute on a stringed or keyboard instrument and audiate while exhaling.

The tongue plays an important role in correctly articulating what is to be performed, because it coordinates the appropriate parts of the body in performance. The child must be taught how to use her tongue not only for the proper articulation of tonal patterns and rhythm patterns on a wind instrument, but also for the proper readiness for audiating tonal patterns as well as of rhythm patterns at a later time.

There are other details that need to be considered before a child is encouraged to begin to take lessons on a music instrument. Readiness associated with personality and emotional characteristics are best assessed by parents. The appropriateness of what and how a child is to be taught is best assessed by a qualified teacher. Many teachers exercise that responsibility by selecting the instructional books that a child will use. An instrumental music series that reflects the philosophy discussed in this chapter is *Jump Right In: The Instrumental Curriculum* (Grunow and Gordon, 1989). *Jump Right In: The Music Curriculum* and *Jump Right In: The Instrumental Curriculum* are designed to coordinate what a child is learning in general music with what she is learning in beginning instrumental music. The teaching procedures employed and the content included in *Jump Right In: The Instrumental Curriculum* are discussed below.

In beginning instrumental music, a child must be taught sound before sign, that is, audiation before notation. First she must develop vocabularies of tonal patterns and rhythm patterns through singing and chanting. Then she can be taught how to play those patterns on an instrument. Finally she should be taught how to read what she can audiate and already play. Music theory, which is actually the theory of how music is notated, should be taught last, if it needs to be taught at all. It is of great importance that the child engage in a continuous process of learning to sing and to chant unfamiliar tonal patterns and rhythm patterns as she is learning to play familiar ones on her instrument.

Having learned to sing tonal patterns with tonal syllables and to chant rhythm patterns with rhythm syllables at the verbal association level of skill learning sequence, a child is able to learn to play those patterns on her instrument. She does not need to be taught the letter names of the lines and spaces of the staff or the time value names of notes. The child is told, for example, that C (the name of a pitch that is heard in audiation and not necessarily the name of a line or space that is seen on the staff) is "DO" and that it is fingered in a specific way. Next she learns, in association with C "DO," how "RE" is fingered, how "TI" is fingered, and so on. It is not necessary for her to learn pitch names associated with syllables other than "DO." In time she learns a number of fingering patterns that may be used when C is "DO." She is then taught the name of and the fingering around another "DO," for example G, and she learns fingering patterns that may be used when G is "DO," and so on. A child experiences far less confusion in learning that "DO" can be found in several places on her instrument (a movable system) than in learning that C, for example, is always referred to and called by the letter name C (a fixed system) regardless of whether it is audiated, for example, as "DO" in one keyality or as "SO" in another. Children are able to learn fingerings rapidly, particularly when a specific fingering is successively repeated as a result of its being used only to perform a given rhythm pattern.

A child should learn to audiate and to perform in different tonalities, such as major and minor, as soon as possible. She should be taught fingerings for one or more pitch names associated with "LA" before she is taught an abundance of pitch names that are associated only with "DO." Also, a child should learn to perform through audiation fewer rhythm patterns in a variety of meters rather than to read many rhythm patterns that are in the same meter but notated with different measure signatures. As soon as feasible, a child should be taught to improvise on her instrument. Ideally, she should learn to improvise before she is taught to read notation.

115

Probably the most important pedagogical practice in teaching a child who is beginning to learn to play a music instrument is often overlooked. The child should be given ample opportunity to hear a professional musician play the instrument that she, the child, is learning to play. Many children have no idea of what an instrument is supposed to sound like until long after they have been playing that instrument. Once a child hears the appropriate tone quality of an instrument, she is able to audiate that quality, and to strive for it in performance. She is also able to profit from hearing good musical phrasing. The opportunity to hear a well turned phrase can be generalized in audiation to all types of music. It would be advantageous for a child to have at her disposal a recording on which the instrument that she is learning to play is played by a professional musician in solo. Such recordings are a constituent part of *Jump Right In: The Instrumental Curriculum.*

GLOSSARY

Acculturation
The first type of preparatory audiation. It includes three stages. Typically children are in the first stage from birth to eighteen months of age, in the second stage from one to three years of age, and in the third stage from eighteen months to three years of age.

Arpeggioed Pattern
A tonal pattern in which almost all of the pitches move by skip, not by step.

Assimilation
The third type of preparatory audiation. It includes two stages. Typically children engage in the assimilation type of preparatory audiation from four years of age to five years of age. Some children may enter the first stage as early as three years of age and the second stage as early as four years of age.

Audiation
Hearing and formally comprehending in one's mind the sound of music that is no longer or may may never have been physically present. It is different from discrimination, recognition, imitation, and memorization. There are seven types and six stages of audiation. Ideally, children begin to audiate when they are five years old.

Classroom Activities
That part of informal guidance or formal instruction during which traditional activities, not learning sequence activities, take place.

Content Learning Sequence
Either tonal or rhythm content used in conjunction with skill learning sequence in learning sequence activities.

Creativity
The spontaneous audiation and use of tonal patterns and rhythm patterns without restrictions.

Developmental Music Aptitude	Innate music potential that is affected by the quality of environmental factors. A child is in the developmental music aptitude stage from birth to approximately nine years of age.
Diatonic Pattern	A tonal pattern in which the pitches move by step, not by skip.
"Do" Signature	That which is traditionally called a key signature. A key signature, however, does not indicate any one keyality or tonality. It indicates only where "DO" may be found on the staff.
Dominant Pattern	One function of tonal patterns. In major tonality it includes an arrangement of the tonal syllables "SO TI RE, FA." In minor tonality it includes an arrangement of the tonal syllables "MI SI TI RE."
Dominant Pitch	The pitch of the fifth degree of a scale.
Duration	A part of a rhythm pattern. A duration is to a rhythm pattern what a letter is to a word.
Formal Instruction	Learning that is imposed upon a child and promotes the development of his senses of objective tonality and objective meter. It usually takes place with children older than five, in terms of audiation, in a school. The emphasis is on cognition and learning what to audiate as well as how to audiate.
Harmonic Minor	A tonality which is established by raising the seventh degree of the minor scale a half step. Harmonic minor and major are fundamental for establishing a sense of tonality. Whenever the word "minor" or the term "minor tonality" is used in this book, harmonic minor is meant.
Idiographic Assessment	Comparing a child to himself. The assessment a child's musical development by comparing his

118

music achievement with his music aptitude or with his past music achievement.

Imitation	The second type of preparatory audiation. It includes two stages. Typically children engage in the imitation type of preparatory audiation from three to four years of age. Some children may enter the first stage as early as two years of age and the second stage as early as three years of age.
Improvisation	The spontaneous audiation and use of tonal patterns and rhythm patterns with restrictions.
Informal Guidance	Learning that is not imposed upon a child, but encourages the development of his senses of subjective tonality and subjective meter. It usually takes place with children younger than five, in terms of preparatory audiation, in the home or in a preschool. The emphasis is on intuition and learning how, not what, to audiate.
Interval	The distance between two pitches.
Key Signature	That which is actually a "DO" signature.
Keyality	The pitch name of the tonic. A keyality is audiated, whereas a key signature is seen in notation.
Leading Tone	In major and minor tonalities, the pitch of the seventh step of the scale.
Learning Sequence Activities	That part of informal guidance or formal instruction during which the practical application of music learning theory is made.
Letter Names	The names of the lines and spaces of the staff.
Macro Beat	The fundamental beat in a rhythm pattern.
Major Tonality	The tonality that has "DO" as the resting tone.

119

Measure Signature	That which is usually called a time signature or a meter signature. A time signature or meter signature, however, does not indicate any one tempo or meter. It indicates only the fractional value of a whole note that will be found in one measure.
Melodic Pattern	The combining of a tonal pattern and a rhythm pattern.
Melodic Rhythm	The rhythm of the melody or the words. It is superimposed upon, and includes divisions and elongations of, macro beats and micro beats.
Meter	That which is determined by the length of macro beats, how macro beats are divided, and how macro beats are grouped.
Micro Beats	The equal divisions of a macro beat.
Minor Tonality	The tonality that has "LA" as the resting tone. Whenever the word "minor" or the term "minor tonality" is used in this book, harmonic minor is meant.
Music Achievement	Accomplishment in music.
Music Achievement Test	A test to measure music accomplishment.
Music Aptitude	The potential to achieve in music.
Music Aptitude Test	A test to measure music potential.
Music Babble	The "musical" sounds young children make before they develop their senses of subjective tonality and subjective meter. It typically occurs from Stage 1 to Stage 4 of preparatory audiation. Music babble is to music as speech babble is to language.

Music Learning Theory	The theoretical explanation of how we learn sequentially when we learn music.
Normative Assessment	Comparing a child with other children. The assessment of a child's musical development by comparing his music aptitude with the music aptitude of other children or by comparing his music achievement with the music achievement of other children.
Pitch	A part of a tonal pattern. A pitch is to a tonal pattern as a letter is to a word.
Pitch Name	A letter associated with a sound of a pitch. Not a letter name associated with a line or space on the staff.
Objective Keyality	A keyality for which there is consensus.
Objective Meter	A meter for which there is consensus.
Objective Tonality	A tonality for which there is consensus.
Preparatory Audiation	Subjectively hearing and informally comprehending in one's mind the sound of music that is no longer or may may never have been physically present. It is the readiness for audiation which a child ideally engages in from birth to five years of age. There are three types - acculturation, imitation, and assimilation - and seven stages of preparatory audiation.
Range	The distance between the lowest and the highest pitches in a song.
Resting Tone	The syllable name of the center of a tonality to which the music gravitates. A tonality has a resting tone and a keyality has a tonic.
Rhythm Pattern	A collection of durations which has unique musical meaning in a given meter.

Rhythm Syllables	Different names, such as "DU" and "DE," that are chanted for different durations in a rhythm pattern.
Stabilized Music Aptitude	Innate music potential that is no longer affected by environmental factors. A child enters the stabilized music aptitude stage when he is approximately nine years old, and he remains there throughout life.
Structured Informal Guidance	Guidance that is based upon a child's natural responses and a specific plan. It occurs in acculturation, imitation, and assimilation, specifically Stages 3, 4, 5, 6, and 7 of preparatory audiation.
Subdominant Pattern	One function of tonal patterns. In major tonality it includes an arrangement of the tonal syllables "FA LA DO." In harmonic minor tonality it includes an arrangement of the tonal syllables "RE FA LA."
Subjective Keyality	A keyality for which there is not consensus.
Subjective Meter	A meter for which there is not consensus.
Subjective Tonality	A tonality for which there is not consensus.
Syntax	The orderly arrangement of pitches and durations which establishes the tonality and the meter of a piece of music.
Tempo	The speed at which rhythm patterns are performed, and the relative lengths of macro beats within and among rhythm patterns.
Tessitura	The range within almost all of the pitches of a song are found.
Time Value Names	The fractional names given to relative durations seen in music notation.

Tonal Pattern	Two to five pitches which collectively have unique musical meaning in a given tonality and a given keyality.
Tonal Syllables	Different names, such as "DO" and "SO," that are sung for different pitches in a tonal pattern.
Tonality	That which is determined by the syllable name of the resting tone. If "DO" is the resting tone, the tonality is major, if "LA" is the resting tone, the tonality is harmonic minor, and so on.
Tonic	The pitch name of the center of a keyality to which the music gravitates. A keyality has a tonic and a tonality has a resting tone.
Tonic Pattern	One function of tonal patterns. In major tonality it includes an arrangement of the tonal syllables "DO MI SO." In minor tonality it includes an arrangement of the tonal syllables "LA DO MI."
Transition Stages	Stages 4 and 6 of preparatory audiation. Also, the time during which the change from informal guidance to formal instruction takes place.
Unstructured Informal Guidance	Guidance that is based upon a child's natural responses and not upon a specific plan. It occurs in acculturation, specifically in Stages 1 and 2 of preparatory audiation.
Unusual Meter	Two types of meter in which macro beats are of unequal length, regardless of whether they are audiated in pairs or more than a pair, or whether they are divided into two or three micro beats.
Unusual Paired Meter	The meter that results when macro beats are of unequal length and are audiated in pairs. Some macro beats are divided into two micro beats, and other macro beats are divided into three micro beats.

123

Unusual Unpaired Meter	The meter that results when macro beats are of unequal length and are audiated in more than a pair. Some macro beats are divided into two micro beats, and other macro beats are divided into three micro beats.
Upbeat	An anacrusis. The preparation for performing a macro beat.
Usual Duple Meter	The meter that results when macro beats are of equal length and are audiated in pairs, and in which each macro beat is divided into two micro beats.
Usual Triple Meter	The meter that results when macro beats are of equal length and are audiated in pairs, and in which each macro beat is divided into three micro beats.
Usual Meter	Three types of meter in which macro beats are of equal length and are audiated in pairs. The macro beats are divided into two and/or three micro beats, depending upon the meter.

BIBLIOGRAPHY

Adler, Mortimer J. *Reforming Education.* New York: Macmillan, 1977.

Andress, Barbara, ed. *Prekindergarten Music Education.* Reston, Virginia: Music Educators National Conference, 1989.

Budd, Malcolm. *Music and the Emotions.* London: Routledge and Kegan Paul, 1985.

Chavez, Carlos. *Musical Thought.* Cambridge, Massachusetts: Harvard University Press, 1961.

Davies, John Booth. *The Psychology of Music.* Stanford: Stanford University Press, 1978.

Deutsch, Diana, ed. *The Psychology of Music.* New York: Academic Press, 1982.

Dowling, W. Jay and Dane L. Harwood. *Music Cognition.* New York: Academic Press, 1986.

Eisner, Elliot W. *Cognition and Curriculum.* New York: Longman, 1982.

Farnsworth, Paul R. *The Social Psychology of Music.* Ames: The Iowa State University Press, 1969.

Gordon, Edwin E. *Musical Aptitude Profile.* Chicago: Houghton Mifflin/Riverside Publishing, 1988,1965.

Gordon, Edwin E. *Primary Measures of Music Audiation.* Chicago: GIA, 1979.

Gordon, Edwin E. *Intermediate Measures of Music Audiation.* Chicago: GIA, 1982.

Gordon, Edwin E. and David G. Woods. *Jump Right In: The Music Curriculum.* Chicago: GIA, 1986.

Gordon, Edwin E. *The Nature, Description, Measurement, and Evaluation of Music Aptitudes.* Chicago: GIA, 1987.

Gordon, Edwin E. *Learning Sequences in Music: Skill, Content, and Patterns*. Fifth Edition. Chicago: GIA, 1989.

Gordon, Edwin E. *Advanced Measures of Music Audiation*. Chicago: GIA, 1989.

Gordon, Edwin E. *Audie*. Chicago: GIA, 1989.

Gould, Stephen Jay. *The Mismeasure of Man*. New York: W. W. Norton, 1981.

Grunow, Richard F. and Edwin E. Gordon. *Jump Right In: The Instrumental Curriculum*. Chicago: GIA, 1989.

Hargreaves, David J. *The Developmental Psychology of Music*. Cambridge: Cambridge University Press, 1986.

Hirsch, E. D., Jr. *Cultural Literacy*. New York: Vintage Books, 1988.

Hodges, Donald A. ed. *Handbook of Music Psychology*. Lawrence, Kansas: National Association of Music Therapy, 1980.

Houle, George. *Meter in Music, 1600-1800*. Bloomington: Indiana University Press, 1987.

Howell, Peter, Ian Cross, and Robert West, eds. *Musical Structure and Cognition*. New York: Academic Press, 1986.

Kerman, Joseph. *Contemplating Music*. Cambridge, Massachusetts: Harvard University Press, 1985.

Laban, Rudolf. *Mastery of Movement*. London: MacDonald and Evans, 1971.

Lundin, Robert W. *An Objective Psychology of Music*. Malabar, Florida: Robert E. Krieger, 1985.

Mursell, James L. *The Psychology of Music*. New York: W. W. Norton, 1937.

Radocy, Rudolf E. and J. David Boyle. *Psychological Foundations of Musical Behavior*. Springfield, Illinois: Charles C. Thomas, 1979.

Revesz, Geza. *Introduction to the Psychology of Music*. trans. G. I. C. deCourcy. Norman: University of Oklahoma Press, 1954.

Schoen, Max. *The Psychology of Music*. New York: Ronald Press, 1940.

Seashore, Carl E. *Psychology of Music*. New York: McGraw Hill, 1938.

Serafine, Mary Louise. *Music as Cognition*. New York: Columbia University Press, 1988.

Shuter-Dyson, Rosamund and Clive Gabriel. *The Psychology of Musical Ability*. London: Methuen, 1981.

Sloboda, John A. *The Musical Mind*. Oxford: Clarendon Press, 1986.

Swanwick, Keith. *Music, Mind, and Education*. London: Routledge, 1988.

Teplov, B. M. *Psychologie des Aptitudes Musicales*. Paris: Presses Universitaires de France, 1966.

Vygotsky, L. S. *Thought and Language*. ed. and trans. Eugenia Haufmann and Gloria Vakar. Cambridge: MIT Press, 1967.

Walters, Darrel L. and Cynthia Crump Taggart ed. *Readings in Music Learning Theory*. Chicago: GIA, 1989.

Whorf, Benjamin Lee. *Language, Thought, and Reality*. Boston: The Massachusetts Institute of Technology, 1956.

Zuckerkandl, Victor. *Man the Musician*. trans. Norbert Guterman. Princeton: Princeton University Press, 1973.

127

Index